This is the story of an attempted *coup d'état* m(
Seychelles, an idyllic but obscure group of i
the time, the attempt made headlines across the world; partly because it involved names still famous or notorious from the mercenary involvement in the Congo in the 1960s; partly because it involved the hijacking of an Air India jetliner; partly because South Africa, the international pariah, was involved; and partly because the incident was perceived as another small skirmish in the Cold War. However, this is more than a behind the scenes account of those faded headlines. It is the story of one individual's personal growth. The author writes, 'I was wounded and captured in the Seychelles. I was severely beaten on a daily basis, stood trial and then was sentenced to death. I eventually served two and a half years in prison, a time, which I value with hindsight because I now realise it was then that I discovered hidden depths in my comrades and myself. I discovered humanity in my jailers and in the president of the Seychelles, whom my group had set out to depose. Cut off from my wife and family, I treasured their support from a distance and today do not for an instant take for granted the strength and joy of a loving family. And I deepened my religious faith, which today lights my path. It seems an odd thing to say, but I owe a lot to that escapade in the Seychelles. I realised how shallow and crass the racial attitudes are that exist in this world we live in. Human courage and kindness, I discovered, knows of no racial barriers. I experienced the unbelievable magnanimity and greatness of spirit of President Albert René, the man to whom I owe my life. I also experienced support from a distance from Archbishop Desmond Tutu, a person I had been conditioned to expect nothing from except hostility. It was an illuminating and humbling experience. I also experienced the fickleness of the apartheid regime. I suppose, it would have been expecting a bit much for them to admit they backed the Seychelles attempt and supplied the weaponry, but as far as I am aware, they subsequently did not stir a finger, officially or unofficially, to ameliorate our condition or secure our release. What they did do was put sinister and unpleasant pressure on my wife, alone in Durban with two young children, for reasons I am still at a loss to understand.'

Aubrey Brooks is a motivational speaker/trainer and life skills coach with a difference. Many people have known him over the years as many things: modern day adventurer, petrol head, and adrenalin junkie to name a few. Between working for a living and running his own successful businesses, he has raced cars, motorcycles, powerboats and ocean going yachts. He obtained a pilot's license, sky dived and spent time in the military, including the elite unit the Rhodesian Selous Scouts. Aubrey was involved in an attempted *coup d'état* that took place nearly a quarter of a century ago on the Seychelles islands. He was wounded, captured, severely beaten on a daily basis; he stood trial, and then was sentenced to death. After serving a number of years in prison, including eighteen months on death row and nine months in solitary confinement, he was given a full presidential pardon and released. His search to understand the meaning of life has led him on an incredible journey, a journey that has taken him to many interesting and unusual places. It has also opened up many wonderful opportunities for him; this has included meetings with many, many really outstanding people; he has looked into religious and spiritual beliefs, visited monasteries and retreats; he has been on self-betterment courses, like Mind Power and the Secret; he has also attended a number of courses like meditation and practical philosophy; everything he has learnt, done and seen, over these years, has brought him to his current understanding of the universe that we live in and how we can and must shape our own future. Aubrey and his family now live happily on the unique, wonderful and scenic Isle of Man, where he has his own events company and is also a motivational speaker and life skills coach.

Death Row in Paradise

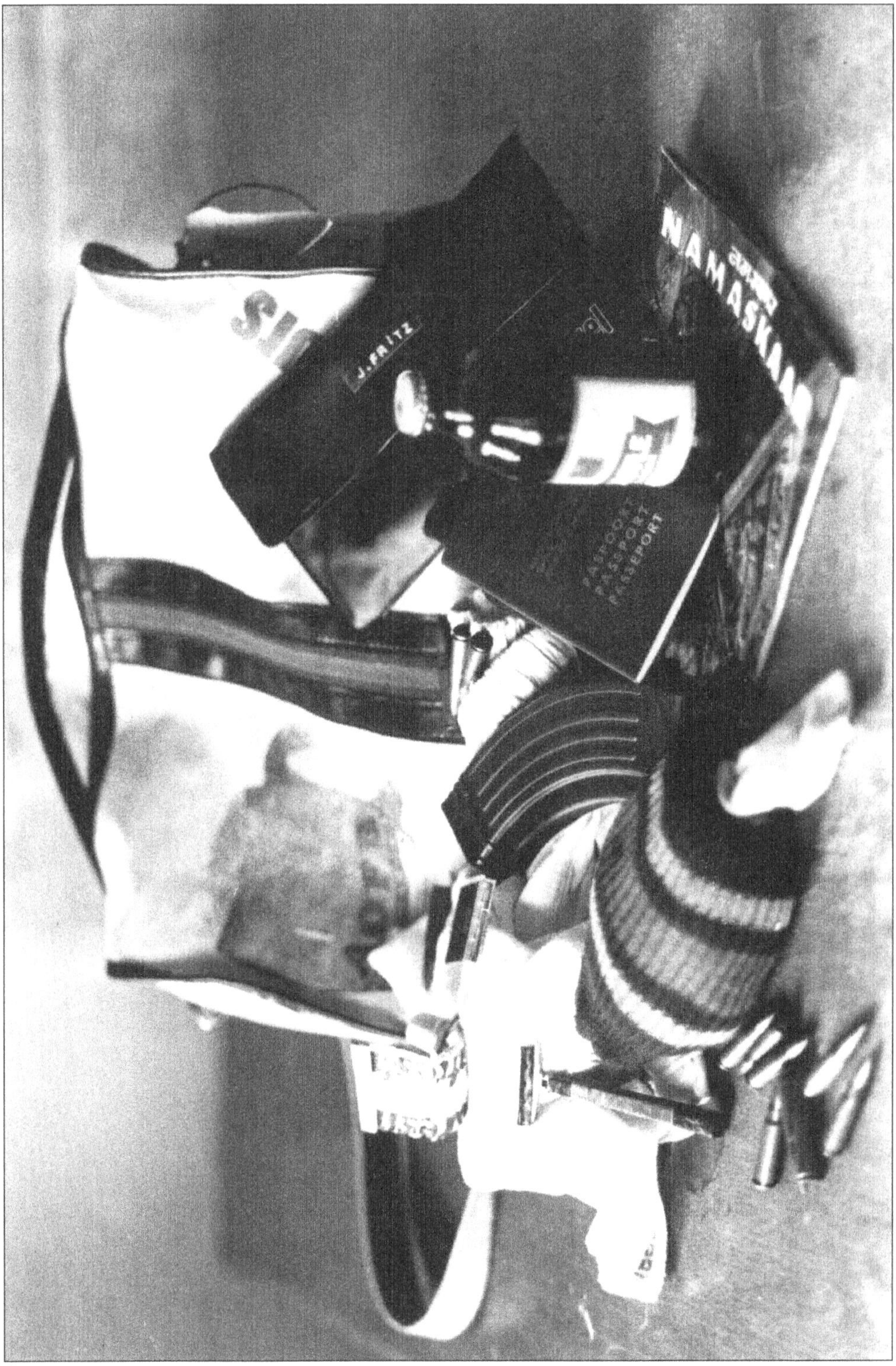
J.FRITZ
PASSPORT
PASSPORT
PASSEPORT

Death Row in Paradise

The Untold Story of the Mercenary Invasion of the Seychelles 1981–83

Aubrey Brooks

HELION & COMPANY

Helion & Company Limited
26 Willow Road
Solihull
West Midlands
B91 1UE
England
Tel. 0121 705 3393
Fax 0121 711 4075
email: info@helion.co.uk
website: www.helion.co.uk
Twitter: @helionbooks
Visit our blog http://blog.helion.co.uk

Originally published by Xlibris 2013

This revised edition published by Helion & Company 2015
Designed and typeset by Peter Johnson, Great White Designs (www.greatwhitedesigns.com)
Cover designed by Paul Hewitt, Battlefield Design (www.battlefield-design.co.uk)
Printed by Lightning Source, Milton Keynes, Buckinghamshire

Text © Aubrey Brooks 2013
Illustrations © private collection

ISBN 978-1-909982-04-8

British Library Cataloguing-in-Publication Data
A catalogue record for this book is available from the British Library

All rights reserved. No part of this publication may be reproduced, stored, manipulated in any retrieval system, or transmitted in any mechanical, electronic form or by any other means, without the prior written authority of the publishers, except for short extracts in media reviews. Any person who engages in any unauthorized activity in relation to this publication shall be liable to criminal prosecution and claims for civil and criminal damages.

For details of other military history titles published by Helion & Company Limited contact the above address, or visit our website: http://www.helion.co.uk

We always welcome receiving book proposals from prospective authors working in military history.

Dedication

My dearest mother Grace, who showered us with much love and affection, she taught us that anything and everything in life, was achievable. And when she felt we were ready, she gently guided us onto the path of life in search of our dreams. Gone but never forgotten.

My most wonderful wife Diane and my family whose love and understanding has been my biggest strength and the inspiration for me to continue on my journey. This has allowed me to live the most amazing and fulfilled life one could ever imagine.

Our extended families, our many friends and their families, my work associates and their families, all the many people and their families around the world that prayed for our return and all the absolutely wonderful people that I have had the pleasure of meeting during this fascinating and enriching journey that I have been on thus far. Thank you all for enriching me, teaching me, understanding me and finally for putting up with me.

Acknowledgements

This book would not have been possible without the help of a large number of people who gave of their time and funds in order to keep our family afloat during the particularly difficult time of my trial, my time in prison and also on my return.

I would like to thank the following people: Diane's parents George and Eve Hinds for supporting and standing by Di and the family (including me) throughout the entire ordeal (which must have been very difficult for them); our defence team, Nicholas Fairburn, Graham Fowlis, Jeremy Ridl and Kieran Shah, who were the most amazing defence team one could wish for (thank you for seeing us home); Graham Linscot for writing this book with me and his great sense of humour; Al Venter and Peter Duffy, for without their guidance I doubt if this book would have gone to press; Dr Dennis Dyer our family doctor and a good friend who was Di's confidant whilst seeing her through the Seychelles saga and for many years after it was all over; Gavin and Rhylda King for taking care of Roy while Di was in the Seychelles for our trial; Kish and Viviene Probert for taking care of our son Roy on numerous occasions; Peggy Cochrane and family for all the support they gave Rory and our family; Alec (Sir Blair) and Evelyn (Mama Luigi) Gibson for being with Di at such short notice, for donning his disguise in venturing out for provisions whilst under siege and their continued love and support; Wally, Lynn, Tessa and Sandy Heales (my god-daughter) for always being there for our family; Andy and May Messina for being there for Di over a very long period; Karen Dalgliesh for being Di's best friend at a time when she was going through her own tough time whilst her husband Ken was imprisoned for the hijacking; James and Michelle Magennis for always being there for us; Mark and Terresa van der Wat for making their cottage available for me and for taking care of me whilst I put the final chapters of the book together, also their daughter Shian (Annie) for her assistance on the computer and Cuwan for his artwork; Pastor Ferdie Warick and the congregation of the Sweetwaters Full Gospel Church in Amanzimtoti for the loan of their recording equipment that was used to record the story whilst it was still fresh in our minds and for their prayers and fellowship; Mrs Engelbrecht who painstakingly transcribed all of the tapes from the recordings; Len Morrison a very good friend for sending me the letter in Appendix 4 (Royal Swazi Airways); and Johnathan Shackleton for all his assistance in restoring and making sure that our photographs were able to be used in this book.

All of the above have been and still remain our very best friends who have continued to support us. This has had a marked influence on our lives for which we are truly grateful.

There are a number of wonderful people that I may have left off the list to whom we will be eternally grateful; you know who you are and I apologise unreservedly for omitting you from these acknowledgements.

Contents

Illustrations	x
Map of the Seychelles	xii
1. The Opening Salvo at the Gate	13
2. The Approach	16
3. Meeting the Colonel and the Briefing	21
4. The Advance Party	28
5. Arrival of the Main Party	34
6. On the Hill and the Arrest	38
7. The Capture and Beatings	43
8. The Move from Pointe Larue Prison	53
9. The Trial	61
10. The Mutiny	71
11. Meeting the President	76
12. The Hijack Trial in Pietermaritzburg	81
13. Life in the Communal Prison	85
14. The Flight to Isle de Platte	88
15. News of our Return to Mahé and the Pardon	99
16. Diane's Story (*by Diane Brooks*)	105
17. The Readjustment	124
18. The Selous Scouts	130
19. The Closing Chapter	133
Appendix I The Selous Scouts	135
Appendix II The Light at the End of the Tunnel	139
Appendix III The Truth Commission Files	147
Appendix IV The Story of Royal Swazi Airways Fokker F28	154

Illustrations

The Battle Plan	26
Passport belonging to Aubrey Brooks	33
Entry stamp	33
The main party disembarking from the aircraft	37
The main party's arrival	37
Sketch by Cuwan van de Wat—the sequence of events after the shootout at the airport	42
Aubrey Brooks shortly after his capture	51
Aubrey Brooks and Roger England on show to the world press	51
Aubrey Brooks and Roger England at a press showing	52
Radio frequencies and type of aircraft to be used for the incoming government	52
Commissioner of Police James Pillay	58
The first remand	59
Going to court for one of the many remand hearings	59
Aubrey Brooks and Barney Carey	60
The last time we appear in court with Susan Ingle	60
Diane Brooks on the first day of the trial	67
Martin Dolinchek and Aubrey Brooks leaving court	67
Aubrey and Diane Brooks	68
Martin Dolinchek and Aubrey Brooks on the way to court	68
Nicholas Fairburn Q.C.	69
Jeremy Ridl and Nicholas Fairburn at the Pirates Arms	69
The death warrant for Aubrey Brooks	70
Sketch by Cuwan van de Wat of our prison (at Unionvale)	75
President Albert René addressing the nation	79
Aubrey Brooks at a press conference	80
In the prison garden on Isle de Platte	96
The six of us on the veranda of our prison home on Isle de Platte	97
The six of us at a press conference on Isle de Platte prior to our release	97
The four of us in our room on Isle de Platte	98
The six of us at police headquarters	103
The four mercenaries (sentenced to death) at a press conference	104
The signed menu from the British Airway's crew on the flight home	104
Diane Brooks in South Africa	122
Diane Brooks awaiting news back home	122
Letter to Di from the British High Commissioner	123
The welcome home for Col. Hoare at Hilton in Kwazulu Natal	129

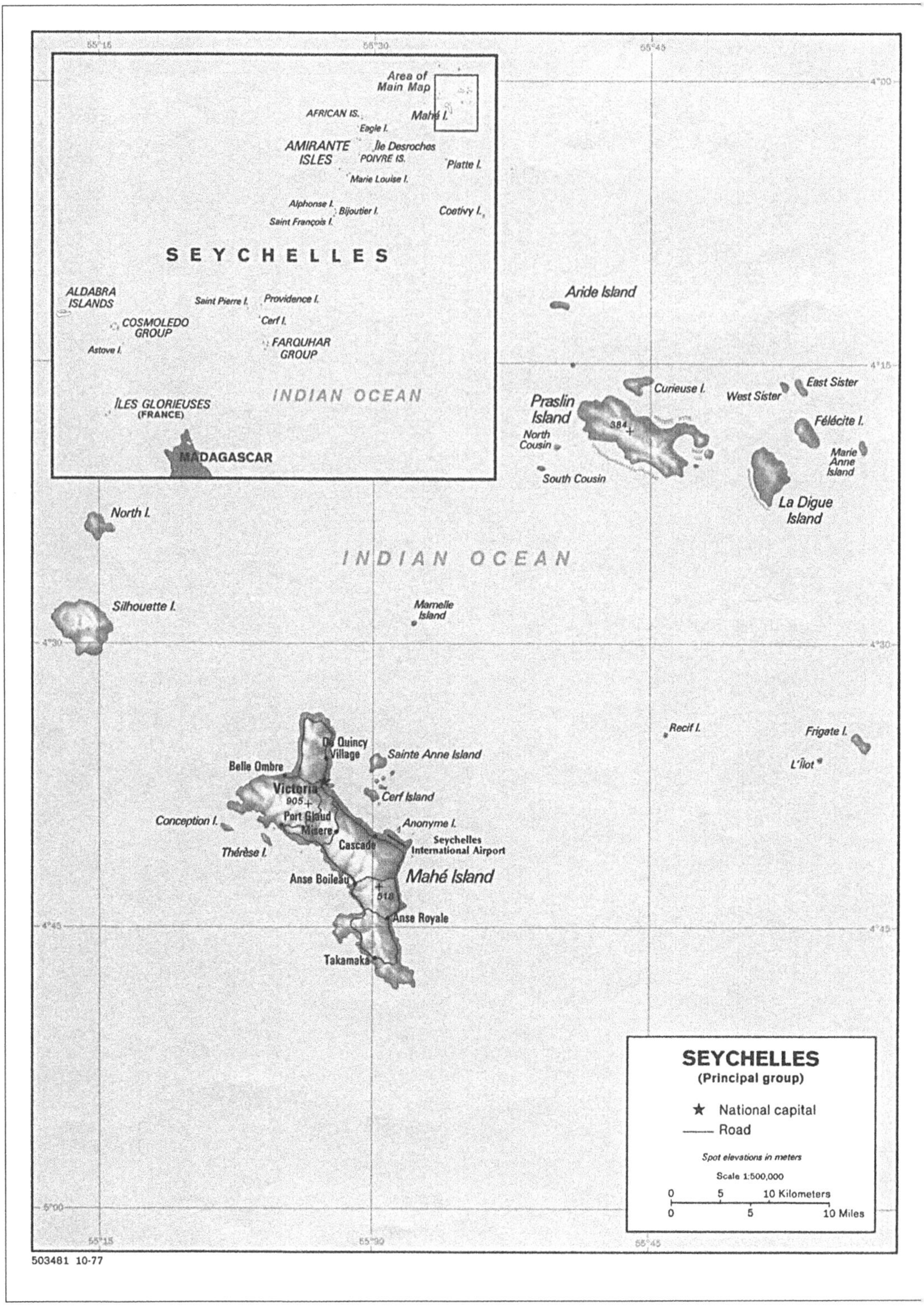
Area of Main Map
AFRICAN IS.
Eagle I.
Mahé I.
AMIRANTE ISLES
Île Desroches
POIVRE IS.
Platte I.
Marie Louise I.
Alphonse I.
Bijoutier I.
Saint François I.
Coetivy I.
SEYCHELLES
ALDABRA ISLANDS
Saint Pierre I.
Providence I.
COSMOLEDO GROUP
Cerf I.
Astove I.
FARQUHAR GROUP
ÎLES GLORIEUSES (FRANCE)
INDIAN OCEAN
MADAGASCAR
Aride Island
Curieuse I.
West Sister
East Sister
Praslin Island
384
Félécite I.
North Cousin
Marie Anne Island
South Cousin
La Digue Island
North I.
INDIAN OCEAN
Silhouette I.
Mamelle Island
Recif I.
Frigate I.
L'Îlot
De Quincy Village
Sainte Anne Island
Belle Ombre
Victoria
905
Cerf Island
Port Glaud
Conception I.
Misere
Anonyme I.
Cascade
Seychelles International Airport
Thérèse I.
Anse Boileau
Mahé Island
518
Anse Royale
Takamaka
SEYCHELLES
(Principal group)
National capital
Road
Spot elevations in meters
Scale 1:500,000
0 5 10 Kilometers
0 5 10 Miles
503481 10-77

1
The Opening Salvo at the Gate

It was like something out of a bad movie. War is not supposed to be like this. Roger, Charlie, Ken and I were going up to the guardroom of the barracks as if we were troopies checking in after a pass. Charlie was holding out an AK 47 to the guy on sentry duty and saying, 'Has anyone lost this?' Yet we were there to take the place, or at least hold the armoury to stop the Tanzanians getting out with weapons to attack the main force. It was unreal, almost embarrassing.

'Don't panic, just put your weapons down and nobody will get hurt,' said Charlie, as I was still getting out of the car. At that, the guy just emptied his magazine at us, firing blindly from the hip. Charlie took one in the left shoulder and I took one in the right thigh. I went down right away and rolled behind the vehicle for cover. I was in a relatively safe position, so I opened up on the guardhouse. I had lost sight of Ken but he was firing from somewhere pretty close by; Charlie was firing from behind the cover of a bush, away to the left; but Roger was standing out in the open exchanging fire with the Tanzanian from about twenty paces, like it was the Gunfight at OK Corral.

'For God's sake get some cover!' I yelled at him. Then he ran across to a little house on stilts beside the driveway and carried on firing from there.

This was a bad situation to be sure, but for the moment I did have good cover under a tree. Nevertheless, we would have to move fast. Any moment the Tanzanians would be pouring out of there, armed to the teeth, with only us – holding the puny, butt-less AK 47s they had equipped us with, along with a few clips of ammunition – standing between them and the main force at the airport. Suddenly my good cover began to disappear as a 14.5 mm anti-aircraft gun opened up on us from within the barracks. My tree was being shredded about my ears; with every loud explosion more of the shrubbery would go walkabout and I was becoming badly exposed. But I kept on firing. I was determined to get the little bastard who had shot me. I could see him there; he was hiding behind a low wall on the veranda, which was in front of the guardroom. He was just shooting bursts randomly in my direction and it was one of those random bursts that he had been firing at Charlie that had hit me in the first place. At this point I was not pleased, but try as I may, I could not hit him. First the rounds would hit the roof above his head and the next they would hit the ground in front of him, sending up little puffs of dust in the process. Those stripped-down AKs had been perfect for close quarters combat, but were pathetic for accuracy.

We then crawled under the stilted house for better cover. That anti-aircraft gun was becoming a menace. Fortunately for us, probably due to a lack of proper maintenance it was jamming every few shots and this gave us a bit of a breather, but it was not nice to have the heavy stuff whining about our ears like that. Time was running out, not to mention ammunition. So we decided to move up the hillside and try to work out a way to get into the base and silence the gun. It was imperative that we seize the armoury and soon; our plans had come badly unstuck but if we could manage that, we were still in with a chance. We could see movement at the back of the barracks, but could not be sure whether it was people being issued with weapons or whether they were running away.

I was making heavy going: my right leg felt numb and I was bleeding badly. But Roger said it was just a flesh wound and he put a tourniquet, torn from my shirt, on my leg. That 14.5 gun was following us up the hillside with its fire, but at least there we had decent cover in the bush. This was more like what we had been used to in Rhodesia. We had just finished the first aid when we spotted Colonel Hoare and Barney Carey, down below on the road quite a long distance away. The Colonel looked cool as a cucumber, still in his blazer, and Barney had what appeared to be a radio. They were directing things, not caring a damn about the bullets that were flying around. We had lost Ken somewhere in the bush and it was getting toward dusk and starting to drizzle. My leg was also beginning to play up worse and worse. This was more than a flesh wound, and I was becoming a hindrance to the party, especially as the hill became steeper. We decided I should go down again and meet up with the main body.

I set off on my own down the hillside, getting cut to ribbons by the thorns, and then I blacked out; I suppose because of loss of blood. I came to, what must have been hours later, woken, I think, by the sound of a large jet coming in to land at the airport down below. There was an absolute din of small-arms fire coming from the airport, as well as the lower slopes of the hill I was on. But you could not tell which side was which. We were all using AKs, not like in the Rhodesian bush where you could always pick out the R1s, R5s or SLRs of our own fellows. There was no way I could get through that lot to the main force. I decided to get higher up the hill again to see if I could make out the lights of the Reef Hotel, where some of our party had been staying. I had to work out some way of getting there and I also needed to get some medication quickly. I guess I did not think far enough ahead. How does one stagger unobserved into a holiday hotel with a gunshot wound, pick up one's key at the desk and go upstairs to call room service for a doctor and a cold beer. This was indeed a pickle. I dropped to my knees and said the Lord's Prayer. I also prayed for deliverance from this mess. I felt calmed and, strange to say, I believe that in spite of what lay ahead, things began to change for me in the long run. It would be a very long run though. Just then a Seychellois and his sister came up the footpath and almost fell over me.

'Stop, stand still and you won't get hurt!' I said.

But the woman started screaming her head off, which was the last thing I needed. Her brother and I managed to quieten her down and they gave me a metal mug, a bottle of orange juice and a piece of cloth, which I made into a better tourniquet. The pair slipped away into the bush, eager to put distance between themselves and the action, because by now bullets and ricochets were beginning to ping through the treetops about us. The orange juice was like nectar. I crawled a distance up the hillside, then found what I thought was a small cave; I quickly squeezed myself in the small space and tried to gather myself. I could see the lights of the Reef Hotel – so near and yet so far – but the airport sector was a complete blackout, from where you could hear a war raging. I pulled my leg up on to the branch of a tree to try to stop the bleeding. I knew that with the possibility of shock setting in, I should not fall asleep. However, it was not too long before I dosed off. I do not know how long I slept for, but I was suddenly awoken by the sound of a big jet aircraft taking off. The noise seemed to drown everything else out. I was not to know it at that time, but it was carrying the main party back to Durban and safety. Nor was I to know that my buddy, Barney Carey, who I had earlier spotted down on the road with Colonel Hoare, had refused to fly back with them and had come to look for me. In fact, he was on the same hill, not all that far from me, and we were about to share the hardship of the next three years in very close proximity. What a guy! Would I have made it without him?

2
The Approach

How did I get involved in this escapade? There were several factors that coincided: I was more or less at a loose end at the time that I was approached to join the operation; I had just been swindled out of a great deal of money; and like many whites in southern Africa – liberals as much as racial hardliners – I was alarmed by what was seen to be communist encroachment in the Indian Ocean and on the east coast of Africa. (It was not all South African government propaganda.) Anything to turn that back just had to be a good cause. But first let me tell a little about my background.

I am a religious man, humble before God. I grew up as a formal Roman Catholic. I was an altar boy and all that kind of thing. I drifted away from the Church as the Bush War developed, because I just could not understand why the Church was sheltering and supporting communist terrorists; this went against everything we were taught to believe. But I did not drift away from God. Right through that terrible Bush War, I never did lose faith and today I wear round my neck the crucifix given to me by my wife, Diane (Di), when I was a prisoner on the Seychelles. Now whenever I worship, I go to whichever church is the nearest. I have also since studied eastern religions and philosophies. I do not pretend to have the answers, but of this I am convinced: we are all answerable to God and in some way, we all worship the same God. I mention this, because religious faith has played a big part in my life and it certainly got me through the rough days, during the Bush War and the Seychelles.

I was born in the old Rhodesia and grew up in Salisbury in fairly privileged circumstances. My father was a successful businessman, although he was a very stern and demanding man. This was balanced out by my mother, also a hardworking person, who showered us with love and a self-belief that we were capable of doing anything and doing it well. As a youngster I used to race powerboats on Lake McIlwaine and go-karts in the junior events at race meetings. I did all right academically at school but, as I grew older I became almost obsessed with sport and did even better there – rugby, cricket, athletics and boxing. Soon after leaving school I became the amateur middleweight champion of Rhodesia. After that I qualified as a printer and worked for a firm in Salisbury. Meanwhile, I took up car racing and rallying, often travelling to events in South Africa and Mozambique, as well as Rhodesia. I gained my private pilot's licence and got very involved in flying. I guess

I was a junkie for the adrenalin rush. That kind of thing needed money of course, but I have always believed in working hard and playing hard. I am a party animal. To fund my racing and flying I had to work much overtime at the printing works. In fact a workmate and I used to vie with each other in setting a new Rhodesian record for overtime worked in the printing industry. Sometimes I would not go home for three days at a stretch. As I say, work hard, play and hard. I have done it all my life.

I moved from the printing trade to join the Rhodesian Broadcasting Corporation, where I received training in master control at the television studios and was stationed in Salisbury. But then opportunities beckoned on Lake Kariba. With my background in power boating, I decided Kariba was the place to be. I moved up there and started a boat hire and lake charter business, serving the tourist trade. There I met all kinds of celebrities – film stars, singers and the like. They were relaxed days. I had a fleet of fourteen boats on the lake. I also had all kinds of sidelines. As international sanctions against Rhodesia developed, I made a pretty good living out of manufacturing, in a small way, all kinds of gadgets we could no longer import. We Rhodesians were pretty resourceful. I think that sanctions in fact opened many business opportunities for a lot of people in Rhodesia.

But during my time at Kariba, the Bush War was beginning to turn ugly. It had been bad enough even before the Portuguese decided to pull out of Mozambique, because they had virtually lost control of the interior by then. It meant our forces had to stage operations deep inside Mozambican territory to strike at terrorist bases and staging posts to try to keep them away from our farming areas in the east and northeast. After the Portuguese left it became worse, desperate really. We had this long frontier to defend, in heavy bush. It would have been bad enough in conventional warfare. In guerrilla warfare you had no option: you had to attack the enemy across the border on his own ground, as far as possible to keep him on the defensive. That was where units like the Selous Scouts came in. Like any Rhodesian man, I was called up for service with the Territorial Army, eventually serving three months on and one month off. I served in the Corps of Signals, where I became a colour sergeant specialising in training. I felt Signals was not quite my bundle and managed to get a transfer to the Police Anti-Terrorist Unit (PATU) stationed at Kariba, where I was living. During this period the Tracker Combat Unit (TCU) was holding selection courses and so I applied. This was more like it. The TCU developed into the Selous Scouts, and after selection I eventually got back my old rank of colour sergeant.

All kinds of experts have written about the Selous Scouts and their role in the war. I am not about to compete with them. All I want to say is that I agree with the view that the Rhodesian special force units were probably the most effective counterinsurgency forces in the world at that time. We were at the sharp end of a very rough and very ugly war, against opponents who had never read the Queensbury Rules. Some nasty things happened, inevitably. I also want to say my conscience is clear. Every operation we conducted – sometimes deep inside Mozambique or Zambia – was militarily necessary and under orders. I never took pleasure out of killing and destruction. Nor did my fellow Scouts, I am sure. But war is a horrible business and, as far as we were concerned, we had not started it. I ended up in the Grey Scouts (the mounted horse unit); this was also an elite counterinsurgency unit.

As far as I am concerned, we never did lose on the battlefield. We lost politically and economically. The ZANU (Zimbabwe African National Union) people feared and hated nobody more than the Selous Scouts. We had been right there at the sharp end. They knew us – we knew them. After Lancaster House, and the election, which was won by ZANU, there was no place in the new Zimbabwe for people of my war background. I was one of the many who were told that it may be in our best interest to look for another place to live. We moved to South Africa. Not so much because we did not believe in the new deal, but because we had no option. Di and I packed the jalopy and headed south with our elder son Rory and baby Roy. I had R900 in my pocket, which was all we were allowed to take with us.

We wound up in Amanzimtoti, a seaside town just south of Durban, in the South African province of Natal. I urgently needed work, partly to pay the rent and support my family and partly to qualify for a residence permit. There was a lot of sympathy in Natal for ex-Rhodesians, who were seen as kith and kin; Natalians also being mainly of British stock. I did not have too much difficulty landing a job in Amanzimtoti as a car salesman. I liked the people who gave me the job. Although I was successful, selling cars was not my bundle. I looked around for something else.

My break came when a small printing works came up for sale at a very reasonable price. I was, of course, a trained printer. It was a small shop just off the Esplanade, in Durban, at the edge of the harbour. I managed to borrow the money from the father of a very good friend. He gave us an incredible amount of support and with that, we threw everything into this venture, all the energy we had. It worked. The business grew fast and I repaid the loan in just a few months. We were working very long hours but making good money. It seemed I was at last carving some sort of spot for myself. The war in Rhodesia was in another life.

Just along the Esplanade from my printing works was the Riviera Hotel, owned by the father of Ken Dalgliesh, a former Rhodesian policeman who had also come south. I often dropped in there for a drink on the veranda. It was a place where I bumped into all kinds of ex-Rhodies. But I never was a 'When-We' (the boring folk who would start a conversation with 'When we were in Rhodesia ...'). All that was in the past; I was making a new life.

However, the growth in my printing business was beginning to present a few problems. The money was good, but it was wearing us ragged. As our business kept expanding, the contracts were getting bigger, then the payments were taking longer and longer to come in. We were very much a one-man show. I had a small staff, but largely it was just Di and me. The actual printing side of it, the sales, the customer relations, credit control, deliveries – all of that was done by us. We were working ridiculously long hours and not spending much time at home. Also, our print shop overlooked the harbour and every day I found myself looking out over one of the most beautiful harbours in the world. Durban harbour comes right into the city;

when you are travelling down the Esplanade in your car, you see ships moving along as if they were in another lane of traffic. They have got a world-class yacht basin and three main yacht clubs. They also have wonderful offshore sailing facilities from where they launch Hobie Cats and other dinghies into the open sea. I began to think along the lines of getting back to something more like what I had been doing at Kariba. The printing business was going great guns. I had the figures to prove it. If I could sell it, I should have enough capital to get back into the boating and leisure business, even if only in a small way. I could get my life back.

I put the word out that I was open to offers. Some folk from a much bigger printing company came down to see me. They looked around and they said they liked what they saw. Then they made me a different proposition: why not merge with them, in return for a senior partner's position and a share in profits? Salaried position! To a refugee from Rhodesia that was bait I could not resist. They talked me into it and my printing equipment got moved up to their plant. For a month or two I was 'happy as larry'. But then it turned out they were a bunch of shysters. Their company was actually on the skids at the time they merged with me. Pretty soon it went insolvent and I lost every cent, not to mention our wasted effort. I was sore, but cowboys do not cry.

You and your family have to eat, so I got a job with an insurance company. I was selling quite a few policies and I did enjoy it, also my boss and my workmates were very nice, but I could not see myself doing this the rest of my life. I was becoming dissatisfied and restless. The bottom had fallen out of things. It was at this time that I was approached about the Seychelles operation. It was not the first time I had had this kind of approach. Africa is a continent of tin pot dictators, civil wars, coups, and mineral exploitation by the multinationals. Mercenaries are often in demand to tip the balance here, hold the line there, prop up so and so in power and protect the expat workers. The money usually comes from the multinationals or from the offshore funds of the particular dictator. It is all very discreet and low-key, and the mercenaries always call an operation like this a 'funny'. People like me with an active military background are always in demand for this kind of thing. During the time I had been in Durban I had been approached at least half a dozen times by people asking if I was interested in a 'funny' somewhere in Africa.

I always turned them down. I was not interested. My Bush War days were over. I had a wife, two sons and all I was interested in was getting my life together. But this time it was a little different. The approach came from Ken Dalgliesh, who was managing the Riviera Hotel for his dad. The man behind it was Colonel Mike Hoare, the legendary mercenary commander in the Congo in the 1960s, who I knew by reputation to be a very honourable man and a highly professional soldier. (He had not been behind any of the other approaches.) I needed the money to make up for what I had been swindled out of in the printing business, so I could make a fresh start. The money on offer was R10,000 for an operation that would be a cakewalk, lasting no more than a few weeks. In 1981, that was an enormous amount. As I say, I was at a loose end, very discontented with what I was doing and I had no doubt at all that the operation would be on the side of the angels.

This was during the Cold War. Soviet and Cuban troops had invaded Angola. The Chinese communists had supported ZANU against Rhodesia, and the Soviets had supported ZAPU (Zimbabwe African People's Union). You read in the papers every other day about the Soviets and the Chinese moving into the Indian Ocean, and it was not just propaganda. This came from serious writers in Britain and the United States. We had all read in the papers about how a left-wing revolutionary in the Seychelles had overthrown a legitimate, elected government and was installing a socialist – for that read communist – dictatorship. We had read how Western interests in the Indian Ocean were threatened: the agreement for the use of the United States' satellite tracking station on Mahé was about to come to an end; South African Airways (SAA) landing rights were about to be stopped (this meant that IATA (International Air Transport Association) could stop the national air carrier – South African Airways – from flying the southern routes); and the naval bunker facilities in Mahé were being used mainly by the Soviet, Indian and other non-friendly fleets. Mike Hoare's operation would obviously be welcomed right across the Western world.

There were four coinciding factors that got me into the Seychelles operation. Firstly, to me, the cause was good. That was a vital factor as I would never get involved in what I knew was a bad cause. If I had not believed in the Rhodesian cause, I am sure I would not have got involved in the war in the way I did. Secondly, there was a good chance of success. I knew of Colonel Hoare by repute. After I had met him and heard him explain the operation, I was sure it would work. There is always an element of risk but that is not the same thing as a scatter-brained operation. I wanted proper military planning and here I had it. Thirdly, I needed the money, as I have explained. Fourthly, I was available. If I had still been running my printing business all hours of the day, I would have had to say thanks, but no thanks. If any one of those four factors had been missing, it would have been thanks but no thanks anyway, the same way it was when the others offered me a funny. I told Ken I was interested but would like to be told a bit more.

3
Meeting the Colonel and the Briefing

The story seems to have got about, that the Seychelles operation was something hatched over the bar counter in the Riviera Hotel in Durban. That is a huge exaggeration; not the whole truth at all. That the Riviera was the haunt of various ex-Rhodies, is true. We used to meet there for a beer or two, which in my case was partly because it was just down the road from my printing works, but mainly because the owner/manager, Ken Dalgliesh, was himself an ex-Rhodie. Refugees hang out together. But it was not the kind of place where things like this were planned. You could not get a crowd of fellows together to talk about something as ultra-sensitive as this. Apart from anything else, the Durban Press Club was on the first floor of the hotel and the last thing we wanted was for the newspapers to get wind of it. However, Ken was well placed to contact ex-Rhodies and it was he who made the initial approach to me, at the Riviera. I suppose it was the same with the other ex-Rhodies who joined. But it was quiet talk out on the veranda, never more than two or three people at a time. When we eventually met Colonel Hoare in Durban for the initial briefing, I did not know half the people present. In the end, half the party were recruited in the Transvaal, and I had never clapped eyes on most of them, either. I do not think Colonel Hoare himself ever set foot in the Riviera. So much for its being the nerve centre of the operation, but it made a good newspaper story (though they never did explain how, if they were such hotshot journalists, something like this could have been hatched right under their noses). Yet it was at the Riviera that I first met Barney Carey. He had just returned from a recce to the Seychelles, where he had taken through immigration and customs, an AK 47 hidden in polystyrene and sewn into the false bottom of his travel bag.

It was an odd thing, but there was an immediate flash of recognition between Barney and me. We both knew we had met somewhere before, and we nodded in recognition before we were introduced, but we never did work out where in the past our paths had crossed. He had been in the Congo with Mike Hoare in the 1960s, but I had not. I had been in the Rhodesian Bush War, but he had not. He lived in Pietermaritzburg, and I lived in Amanzimtoti. Yet somehow we knew each other, even before we knew each other's names. I am not into this stuff about previous existences, but all the same it was puzzling, especially looking back now at the hardships and camaraderie that lay ahead of us both. Maybe a premonition?

There was quite a buzz now in the ex-Rhodie community. A funny was on the go. You could sense some sort of countdown. Nobody knew quite where it would be (though Barney obviously must have, as he had been to the Seychelles on a recce) and there were all kinds of to-ing and fro-ing about who was available and who was not, who was reliable and who was not. Eventually, those of us who had been approached got the word that Colonel Hoare would meet us at suite 19 at Coastlands, a block of holiday apartments near South Beach in Durban, from 2 pm on November 14 (1981). We were to arrive unobtrusively, in pairs.

It was a typical sunny and quiet Saturday afternoon in Durban, and I arrived there with Ken. A small group of fellows were in the apartment, some of whom I knew from the Riviera, but others were total strangers. Colonel Hoare was standing to one side. My initial impression was one of surprise at his smallness of stature; I had always imagined him to be a big, hefty fellow, but actually he was small and wiry. Yet when he started addressing us I realised this was actually a giant of a man, a real officer and a gentlemen, who put his points across with absolute clarity and had a total grip on the situation. As I say, I had said I was interested in the operation, but that I wanted to know more. The Colonel spelt it out: we would be re-installing a legitimate elected president who had been deposed by Marxist revolutionaries on the 5 June 1977; we would have the element of surprise; the opposition would be weak; a majority of the citizens were unhappy that their children were being subjected to compulsory youth camps that taught them not only some skills, but also basic military training; there would be popular support for us; and the whole exercise would be over in a few weeks. I knew this was for me. When you have been on as many military operations as I have, you recognise officer quality when you see it: the way he ticks off every item, every possibility, and the way he keeps cool about it. You just know when you have got quality leadership. That is how I felt about Colonel Mike Hoare, who I had only just met.

Before precisely identifying our target, Colonel Hoare said this was the time for anyone who had misgivings about the operation to say so and withdraw. Only one did. I think he was an officer with one of the local regiments (which are also good units); he said he would not be available for this kind of thing, but he thanked the Colonel all the same for inviting him. Then he withdrew. After that, the Colonel unrolled a map of the Seychelles, a tropical island group in the Indian Ocean populated by Madagascans, Indians and Creoles. They had formerly been a French possession then latterly British.

At this point a detailed battle plan was produced and the discussion of the way forward began.

'Gentlemen this is the objective,' said the Colonel. At which point he told us that a safe house had already been established on Mahé, the main island (in fact it turned out that Bobby Simms, Colonel Hoare's brother-in-law, and Susan Ingle had gone ahead a few months before to set it up) and that it already had a small stock of weapons, which had been smuggled in through customs and immigration. He went on to explain that an advance party of six would arrive in the islands as businessmen and tourists to reconnoitre and check the intelligence provided by the underground resistance movement (Mouvement Pour La Résistance/MPLR). The advance party would also be at the airport, armed, in case anything went wrong while the main party were arriving and a diversionary attack became necessary. The advance party would arrive about a week earlier in order to do their recces and prepare for the arrival of the main party. This was going to be a group of ten; however, the Colonel eventually cut it down to six, as he said the bigger group could become more noticeable. The main party were to arrive on a charter flight from Swaziland, posing as members of the Ancient Order of Froth-Blowers, a charity organisation which combined good deeds with heavy partying. The cover was that they were in the Seychelles to play a game of rugby, get tanked up and distribute toys to orphanages. There actually had been a charity organisation by such a name in England, but I am not sure that it ever existed in South Africa. Colonel Hoare localised it and had silver lapel pins made, as well as specially labelled travel bags. These Froth-Blowers would bring toys and gifts; many were old hands at getting tanked up. But each also had an AK 47 concealed in the false bottom of his travel bag, beneath the toys. People always ask me why we did anything as risky as this. What invasion force has ever brought in its weapons through customs and immigration? Why were they not secretly landed by sea? Durban has hundreds of yachts and trawlers that would have been available. I was not involved in the planning, but I understand the original idea was for a full-on amphibious night assault from the sea, using zodiac rubber boats. This was downscaled from bringing the weapons in the fuel tanks of a yacht (this was too expensive – hire of skipper +/- R100,000, yacht R40,000), to stockpiling arms landed from the sea, then eventually to the suitcase tactic. As I understand it, funding was always a problem. The money available kept getting pared down. Also, there was an anxiety that the regime was about to replace the Tanzanian troops, who were on the island to prop up René's government, with Koreans or Cubans. The project was running out of time. Also, there was a desire to stage the coup at a time, fast approaching, when President Albert René would be on a visit to Paris, just as he had staged his coup while President James Mancham was away at a Commonwealth conference. Everything seemed to be in a rush. It was a matter of only weeks from the time Ken first approached me, to when we were actually on the island. To hide weapons in our luggage was a risky tactic, sure. But Barney had already got them through that way in two test runs. There seemed no reason why our advance party, and the main party, should not get away with it as well.

We then went into more detail about the operation. We discussed the battle plan (although this consisted of numbers and not names); how we were going to approach the objective; we went over the intelligence; discussed the quality of information that we had received; how much we could rely on the local resistance movement; and where we would concentrate more time to double-checking the intelligence that was already on hand. Then all that remained for us to do was to sign the contracts, indemnity forms and that kind of thing. At that point each of us was paid R1,000 cash in a down payment. The rest we were to get on successful completion of the operation, because it would come out of the Seychelles treasury.

Newspaper reports that we were diddled out of our money in the end are absolute trash. That always was the agreement – R1,000 down and the rest when we had staged a successful coup. Then home James!

A week later on 20 November we had a second meeting back at Coastlands and while Colonel Hoare was briefing us, a Seychellois named Gerard Hoareau arrived. I gathered he was a leading light in the exiled section of the resistance movement. He unrolled a poster type document which contained photographs of the Seychelles political power structure, the ruling junta, or whatever it was; it had big crosses across the faces of the president and certain henchmen, who, he said, would have to be 'dispensed with' – I think that is the expression he used. I felt a bit uneasy at this. Colonel Hoare had spoken about a bloodless coup – or as near as possible – yet this guy was talking about rubbing out civilians, and firing squads. This was definitely not my bundle. I sensed other people were feeling the same. Then suddenly Hoareau was out of the place as quickly as he had arrived and Colonel Hoare spoke quietly and seriously about what the man had just said. 'There is absolutely no question of our eliminating political figures,' he said. 'I will not have my hands tainted by their blood. We will do no more than arrest and imprison them.' He went on to add, 'It would be for the incoming government to decide what should be done with them.'

The incoming government was, I believe, due to have been flown in from Kenya only an hour or so after we took over and they would have been bolstered by between 70 and 80 troops or police. Colonel Hoare said he was convinced the Seychellois would not opt for violence and executions. That made us feel better, and I think he was right. Knowing the islands as I now do, the only violent people on them were the Tanzanians. We then once again re-checked the details of the operation; looked at the battle plan in more detail; had another fresh look at how we could best achieve our objective, was it workable; and we also re-visited the intelligence and the information that we had already received, did it ring true, how strong was the local resistance movement. We were then asked if we needed a quick refresher on the AK 47, to which I replied no, as I did not think it was necessary; however, someone said yes and with that a rug was produced and unfurled onto one of the tables. In the middle lay the weapon we were going to use for the operation ahead. At first glance it looked very different: the extra grip that replaced where the hand guard had once been made it look more compact and my thoughts were that this would be a good weapon at close quarters. Anyhow we had a quick run through and everyone seemed to be happy with the weapon of choice. The last item on the agenda that afternoon was the tapes. There were two tapes and one of my tasks was to play these on air at the radio station once the operation was successful. The tapes had to be played at different speeds i.e. so many feet per minute, the order of play, etc…

That was about it. A few of us went across the road to the Lonsdale Hotel, where we met up with Barney's wife, Sandra. With us were Ken, Mike Webb, and Des Botes the karate expert. We had a few quiet drinks, then left just as quietly. The show was getting on the road. I was part of the advance party and was due to fly out the next day. The butterflies were beginning, the way they always do before a boxing match, a motor race or any military op. The adrenalin was starting to pump. Since the last meeting we had only had a week to arrange our air tickets, hotel bookings, travellers' cheques and things like international driving licences. The latter were needed so that we could hire cars on the island in order to carry out our reconnaissance. It had passed in a blur. There were now six of us in the advance party, four to leave tomorrow, Sunday 21, and the other two the day after, Monday 22. We were to fly to Seychelles via Johannesburg. We had good cover stories: Ken Dalgliesh was planning to sell the Riviera Hotel and buy another hotel in the Seychelles; I was his pal, just along for the ride; Barney had some business deal; Des was there to try to mend a broken heart, and to back it up he had in his pocket a Dear John letter from some bird. (Des is actually a natural actor as well as a karate expert. He barely touches a drop of alcohol, yet by the time he reached immigration at Mahé airport he gave the impression of being drunk as a skunk, he was so heartbroken.) Arriving next day were Roger England and Charlie Dukes. Apart from Ken and me, we were all booked separately on the flight and into different hotels.

Come the day and Di took me down to the airport along with our two sons Rory and Roy. She knew that I was about to do another funny and her only stipulation before we knew where the operation was, that it should not be Zimbabwe, because there I could get the death penalty for treason (being a citizen). How prophetic this was to be. On arrival at the airport we met a few of our friends. We also found the rest of the party hanging around, Ken looking splendid in a brand-new Hawaiian shirt and dazzling white flannels. I am sure it looked the genuine thing, a bit of business and pleasure. We then checked in our luggage, which was to go straight through from Durban to Mahé, AK 47s and all. The farewells and goodbyes were said and finally we were off. The operation had started.

In Johannesburg the butterflies started in earnest. Our flight to Mahé was unaccountably delayed by over an hour. Had the weapons been discovered in our luggage? It seemed this could be likely. With every announcement over the public address system we expected to be called to report to airport security. We had with us a Johannesburg telephone number, which we were to call if anything of the kind happened. We were to just give our names, say where we were and what had happened, then hang up. Then everything would be sorted out for us. I have no doubt that on the other end of the line would have been either BOSS (Bureau of State Security – the intelligence agency for the South African government) or Military Intelligence. Barney and I were weighing up this option, when suddenly our flight was called. It transpired that there had been some electrical fault on the aircraft that delayed things.

The six and a half hour flight turned out to be great fun. Ken and I 'met up' with Barney and Des on board, as if it were perfectly natural, and then all of us got into jolly conversation with two married couples who were heading for the Seychelles, one of them on honeymoon. The French do things in style. When the captain heard there was a honeymoon couple on board, he insisted on personally bringing them a bottle of champagne (though the lady in question nearly made a faux pas by mistaking him for the chief steward). Talk was becoming animated. Everyone knew there had been a coup in the Seychelles a couple of years earlier. There had always been some general anticipation of a counter-coup. I gulped inwardly when the honeymoon lady, Colette, remarked, 'Wouldn't it be exciting if there's another coup while we are there and all of us are involved?' Somebody quickly changed the subject.

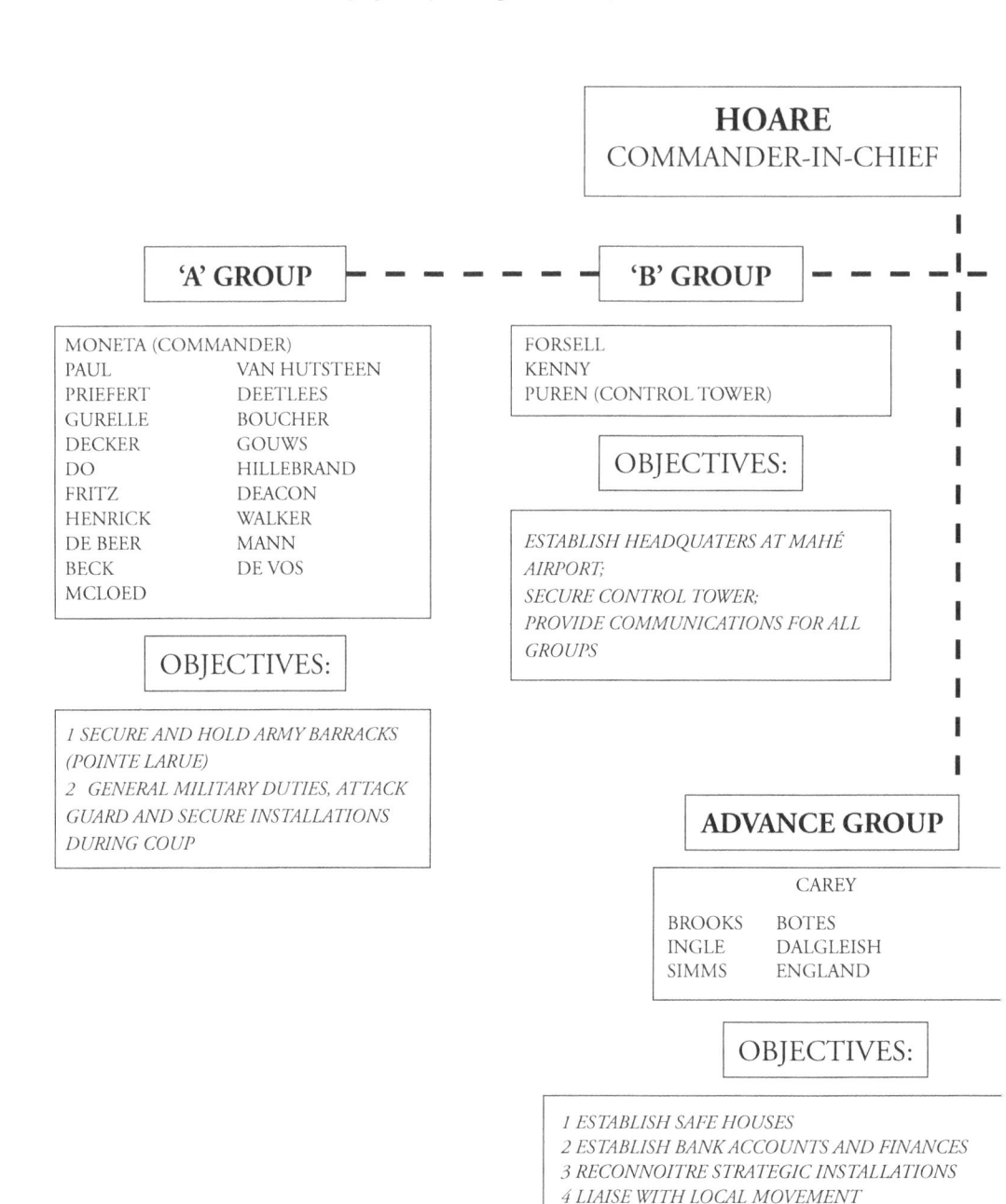

HOARE
COMMANDER-IN-CHIEF

'A' GROUP

MONETA (COMMANDER)
PAUL   VAN HUTSTEEN
PRIEFERT   DEETLEES
GURELLE   BOUCHER
DECKER   GOUWS
DO   HILLEBRAND
FRITZ   DEACON
HENRICK   WALKER
DE BEER   MANN
BECK   DE VOS
MCLOED

OBJECTIVES:

1 SECURE AND HOLD ARMY BARRACKS (POINTE LARUE)
2 GENERAL MILITARY DUTIES, ATTACK GUARD AND SECURE INSTALLATIONS DURING COUP

'B' GROUP

FORSELL
KENNY
PUREN (CONTROL TOWER)

OBJECTIVES:

ESTABLISH HEADQUATERS AT MAHÉ AIRPORT;
SECURE CONTROL TOWER;
PROVIDE COMMUNICATIONS FOR ALL GROUPS

ADVANCE GROUP

           CAREY
BROOKS   BOTES
INGLE   DALGLEISH
SIMMS   ENGLAND

OBJECTIVES:

1 ESTABLISH SAFE HOUSES
2 ESTABLISH BANK ACCOUNTS AND FINANCES
3 RECONNOITRE STRATEGIC INSTALLATIONS
4 LIAISE WITH LOCAL MOVEMENT

The Battle Plan

'C' GROUP

WEBB (COMMANDER)
HEAN   BARNES
WILLAR   DU TOIT
MCKAY   STANDISH-WHITE
GRIBBEN   ROHWEIN
DUFFY   JONES-DAVIES
PRINSLOO   SYDOW
GOATLEY   WILSON
BIDDLECOMBE   DE WET

OBJECTIVES:

SECURE AND HOLD RADIO STATION
SECURE ARMY CAMP ABOVE RADIO SEYCHELLES

'D' GROUP

CAREY (COMMANDER)
BROOKS
BOTES
DUKES
KELLY
DALGLEISH
GREENHALG

OBJECTIVES:

SECURE AND HOLD STATE HOUSE
SECURE CABLE & WIRELESS
SECURE HARBOUR
SECURE AND HOLD CENTRAL POLICE HEADQUARTERS
SECURE AND HOLD ARMY CAMP ABOVE RADIO SEYCHELLES

5 PROVIDE COVER FOR MAIN BODY ON ARRIVAL AT AIRPORT
6 ESTABLISH ACCOMMODATION AND TRANSPORT FOR RESISTANCE MOVEMENT MAIN BODY

4
The Advance Party

It was already dark when we were told to buckle up for landing, and not long after the wheels bumped down gently on Mahé. I had been a little light-headed with the in-flight drinks, but as I took in the whizzing lights along the runway, which gradually slowed, I cleared up fast. This was our objective. This was for real. I had to get through customs and immigration with a false-bottomed bag that contained an AK 47 and ammunition; I was not sure what else could be in the bag. There were the usual pleasantries with the cabin crew as we left, and I felt a little uneasy (it had been some time since I was last on an operation like this). As I stepped out of the cabin on to the stairway, I was struck full in the face by the moist tropical night air that just had a hint of saltiness in it.

Ken and I queued in the arrivals hall, with just that little touch of apprehension to add to the tiredness and anti-climax that follows a long air flight. At an immigration desk, an officer was helping Des Botes to fill in his form. (He was playing to the full his role of a heartbroken inebriate.) Ken and I went through without any hold-up whatsoever.

'Enjoy your stay M'sieur Brooks,' the Creole official said as he stamped my passport.

'I'm sure I will.' I nodded in return.

Then I (along with my bag containing the AK 47) had to get through customs. The customs officers seemed to be examining luggage at random. Just ahead of me in the queue, were a minister of religion and his wife (they too, had just got married and little did I know that many years later I would end up training in a gymnasium that he (Willie) owned). They had to open their bags and the customs officer riffled through them. I felt my palms go clammy. But he waved me through. Shortly, Ken and I were outside the airport building, getting our bags loaded on to a minibus by a jolly Seychellois, who just threw them on the roof without a care (at least the AKs were not assembled or loaded). Before long we were bowling through the night along narrow, twisting roads with sudden jarring as we struck potholes. The route seemed to take us right over the mountain, and the speed the Seychellois drove at was a little hair-raising. But at least we were headed for a shower, a meal and a comfortable bed. It had been too easy… I almost wanted to laugh. Ken and I were booked into the Beau Vallon Bay Hotel; Barney was in the Coral Strand; Roger

England and Charlie Dukes were due to arrive the next day and were booked into the Reef Hotel. We were scattered about, but some of us had already met on the plane and it was only natural we should hang around together.

The next day we hired a car and started on our recce work, but carefully blending in with the normal things tourists would do. We also met up with people we had met on the flight who had nothing to do with our mission. It just made the thing seem more natural and innocent, and in fact we were enjoying ourselves like tourists. Sometimes you had to remind yourself what you had come here to do. We were mainly involved in verifying the intelligence supplied by the Seychellois resistance movement: troop numbers and deployment, police numbers and their location. I had to check out the radio broadcast station, which was my one of my key objectives. Once we had captured the barracks and the armoury, we then had to take the radio station, where I was to air the tapes that had been prepared in advance. They were to be played at fifteen feet and seven and a half feet a minute respectively; these would announce the counter-coup and the return to power of President James Mancham. Within an hour or so, the new government was to arrive by air from Kenya, to be welcomed by jubilant crowds in the streets. We also had to check on the presence, or otherwise, of Soviet and Chinese forces.

The information supplied by the resistance seemed pretty accurate. There were about 200 Tanzanian troops on the islands; most of them were at Pointe Larue, the main barracks near the airport, and they were only issued with weapons from the armoury there, as the need arose. The barracks also had a couple of armoured cars. There certainly were Russians on the island, but they were mainly construction workers. Similarly the Chinese appeared to be building a school or polytechnic. We built up a good picture over the next several days. The Seychelles archipelago is made up of a group of 115 very diverse islands that are scattered about like an assortment of jewels the middle of the azure blue waters of the Indian Ocean and it has some of the most unspoilt tropical hideaways in the world. Looking at the beauty that surrounded us, it was difficult to marry it to the picture of the soldiers always lurking and loitering about the place. This only confirmed what we had been already told (about the presence of the Tanzanians). Anyhow we had come to change things somewhat and this gave us a good feeling for the task that lay ahead. In order to maintain our cover we mixed up our intelligence gathering with a fair amount of tourist stuff like snorkelling and swimming in the wonderfully clear water, where the coral reefs were simply alive with colourful tropical fish. During these fun interludes we mingled with genuine tourists and partied with them. I think some of us genuinely forgot for a second or two about the job at hand. We came across the topless bathing beach; this too was another new experience for an ex-Rhodie, and this was sensational! The whole island was idyllic: palm-fringed beaches, including the famous Coco de Mer (Sea Coconut), with their fruit that suggests women's erotic bits; beaches that shelved so gradually you could walk out into the sea a couple of miles at low tide before reaching deep water; inland, a patchwork of small farms growing sugar, coffee and other crops, interspersed with lush tropical bush; picturesque little Creole houses; and quaint, crumbling Victorian buildings.

The very first evening, Ken and I had arranged to meet up with Barney at the Takamaka Room, which was a kind of sleazy and dingy nightclub that all the tourists go to. There, we sat and chatted quietly for a bit about our mission and what each of us had to do. We were low-key, at the end of the bar, and nobody could possibly have overheard us, what with the music and the din of conversation.

Next thing there was a bit of a disturbance, and we looked up to see a rather burly, very loud character had arrived. He was three sheets to the wind and talking very loudly and aggressively. When he saw us strangers he lurched across and asked where we were from.

'Bring my South African friends drinks!' he roared. 'One day my brother will be back in power and the South Africans will help us do it!'

We just about froze with horror. This turned out to be Frank Mancham. He was indeed the brother of the deposed president that we intended re-installing; he was aggressive, very loud, fairly inebriated and he was seeking out our company. He even started yelling about the need for mercenaries to come in and take out the René government. We just could not believe it. A short while later, the police arrived in the bar and hustled him out. But not before he stripped off his shirt to prove he was not carrying a gun. We were horrified, but the police did not give us a second glance. It seems this behaviour was pretty normal on Frank Mancham's part, and the tolerant, good-humoured way the police handled the incident reinforced an idea, which had been growing in my mind as we visited the shops and eating-places and the other tourist haunts, that the Seychellois were a very laid-back, gentle people who would not hurt a fly. But our mission was not against them, of course; it was against a bunch of communists who had violently and illegally seized power.

Over the next few days we were to make our acquaintance with another very odd character. Colonel Hoare had told us before we set out that a BOSS agent would also be on the island and that he had muscled his way in by assisting with some items for the operation. He would play no role in the mission and would not even contact us. Fat chance! This character got into our hair from the start. He went by the name of Anton Lubic and he was also there posing as a tourist, though his real name turned out to be Martin Dolinchek. This man was a caricature, like something between Inspector Clouseau and Walter Mitty. He could not have been more conspicuous if he tried. It was not just the white flannels, red shirt and white baseball cap – he was forever peering round corners, peeping through curtains, jumping away when anyone approached, taking notes, crouching behind things and creeping through the shrubbery. He used to get incoherently drunk at night. He was a weirdo, the one man on the island you could not help noticing. This Dolinchek came to our hotel, a terrible security risk. He seemed to have paranoia about communists. He saw a Russian or a Chinese behind every bush. He sent us off on a number of wild goose chases, claiming Russian troops had infiltrated a particular civilian project or were at such and such a place or that the Chinese troops were at the next one. We had to check it out every time, and it was complete nonsense. He lived in a fantasy world. Apart from this being highly irritating and a waste of time, he was, as I say, a security risk. We decided to approach Colonel Hoare about him as soon as he arrived, and ask for Dolinchek to be shipped out. In fact if need be, both Barney and I had already decided that if it became too serious, he should be disposed of.

We had completed our recce and everything seemed as it should be. With the element of surprise, Pointe Larue barracks, the main concentration of Tanzanian troops near the airport, should be a pushover. We would have only about forty armed men, but if we moved in quickly, and decisively followed the plan and took the armoury, the operation would be over in next to no time. The idea was that the Froth-Blowers would stick to their cover until zero hour – this would probably be the following Wednesday or Saturday. It was highly likely that the strike would be on the Saturday afternoon, as this would take place while the majority of the army and a lot of the population were at a football match (a very popular pastime on the island). The plan from there was that, once we had wrapped things up, Kenyan troops would arrive from the mainland to take over and we would then quietly disappear. Meanwhile, we were to be at the airport unobtrusively, with our weapons, just in case something went wrong as the main force were flying in. If something out of the ordinary was taking place that could jeopardise the mission (e.g. if there was a larger than normal amount of troops or police about etc.), we would be in a position to create a diversion by firing a number of rounds off at the barracks, driving off, ditching our weapons in the sea and then quietly melting back into our roles as tourists. In the meantime the activity at the airport would be a sign for the aircraft to abort the landing and head back to South Africa.

Perhaps it was an unlucky omen. The night before, Ken went down with terrible gyppo guts. He went pale as a sheet and started sweating and shaking between terrible bouts of diarrhoea and vomiting. The next morning he was still sick as a dog and I told him he had better stay behind. But by lunch he had improved a bit and said he would come along. Some of the group spent the morning snorkelling at a reef (it really is unbelievable, not unlike swimming in a very large pristine aquarium and there used to be a resident manta ray in one of the bays, which was enormous and the first time you got sight of this magnificent sea creature, its size and grace was almost heart stopping). We all returned back to the hotel by lunchtime and then had a braai (Southern African term for a barbecue) – the last bit of steak some of us were to have for a very long time – we then assembled our weapons in the hotel room and clipped in the ammo. We put them in bags in the car boot, covered them with beach gear and set out for the airport to meet the flight, which was due between 3.00 pm and 3.30 pm.

When we arrived at the airport, Bobby Sims was already there, also Martin Dolinchek. Bobby had Dolinchek's weapon in the boot of his car because Dolinchek – being the awkward cuss he is – had hired a Mini Moke instead of a normal car and this vehicle was completely open and had no boot. But it was an anti-climax. The flight was delayed until 5.00 pm, so we dispersed and did a last-minute recce of the barracks and the radio station, just in case anything had changed. Then Ken, Barney, Des and I went to the Reef Hotel for tea and buns, after which Des and I had a quick game of tennis (my first international tennis match?). By this time the butterflies were working overtime. Had our boys been rumbled in Swaziland? Whatever, we did not like the delay. These unexpected delays always tend to get the mind racing off on another tangent – Plan B etc. Soon enough we were back at the airport doing one quick final check on our way – still all was well. Our group sat around drinking tea or beer in the cafeteria and at this point we were all fairly relaxed. At about 05:30 in the evening the Air Swaziland flight came in, and before long the Froth-Blowers were filing through immigration, then customs. The butterflies had disappeared. The game was on. It was like when the bell goes for the first round in a boxing tournament, as you get up out of your corner, the plan goes into action and your mind takes over. I got up and strolled outside. The Froth-Blower's bags were already being piled on the buses, AKs, ammo and all. I spotted a couple of blokes I had been with in the Rhodesian Bush War, and there was a flash of recognition but nothing more, no greeting. It was good to see they were still professionals. Barney and I waited at the door for Colonel Hoare, to give him a lift to his hotel. We had just asked him to give us a few moments, while I told the fellows in the cafeteria to break up and get back to their hotels, when there was a commotion inside the terminal. I heard a woman yell something and then a shot rang out. Suddenly, she appeared out of nowhere and came running past us shouting, 'He's got a gun. He's got a gun.'

THE ADVANCE PARTY

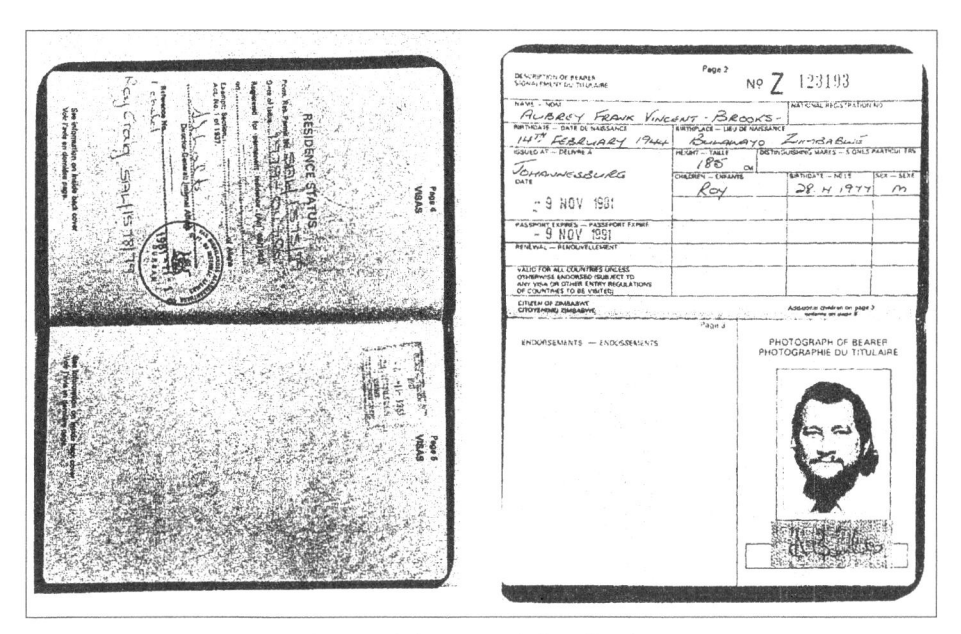

Passport belonging to Aubrey Brooks

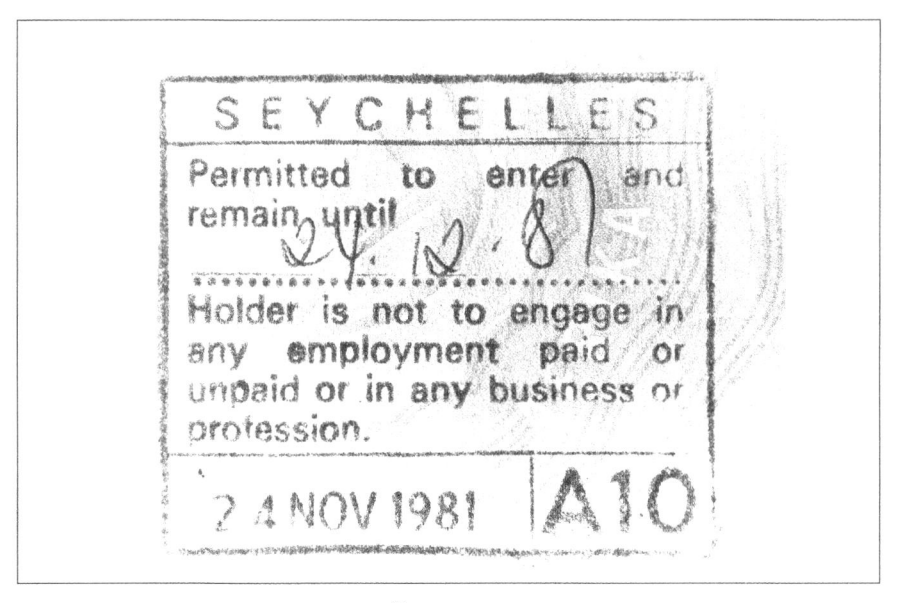

Entry stamp

5
Arrival of the Main Party

This was where our plan unravelled. It actually began on the Royal Swazi Airways flight when it put down at Moroni, in the Comores; there, three travellers left the aircraft and another passenger and one of the airline's staff joined the aircraft (a sixty seat Fokker F28) on its twice weekly scheduled flight to Seychelles. It was felt that this could only add to the cover of the Froth-Blowers mission. Sadly, the French passenger had litchis (a type of fruit) in his baggage and had ignored the in-flight warning of the stewardesses that it was illegal to take fruit into the Seychelles. This was cruel fate. Also, unfortunately, one member of the main party, from the Transvaal contingent, had disobeyed orders by assembling his AK and placing it in the normal luggage part of his bag, he thought this would be a clever idea in case things should go wrong and it was needed in a hurry. (Talk about irony.) We were not to know it, but the trap was sprung and baited.

Colonel Hoare and most of the main party had already passed through immigration and customs, and their bags were being loaded on to the hotel vehicles. The baggage had been opened at random and looked at superficially, most of the customs officers being amused by the squeaky toys and things they found. Colonel Hoare suggests in his book, *The Seychelles Affair*, that the resistance had organised for their supporters to be on duty in customs that day. I would not know about that, but it certainly went very smoothly until one of the officers found the bunch of litchis in the French person's luggage. There was a bit of a noisy altercation and the litchis were confiscated. Then a customs supervisor (not a resistance supporter according to the Colonel's account) insisted that all the remaining bags be properly searched. They take fruit regulations seriously in the Seychelles.

As luck would have it, next in line was none other than our man with his already assembled AK. If the litchis caused a fuss, when they found the AK the customs officers went into orbit. But not for the reasons you might think. If it had not been so bloody serious for us, it would have been comical. The customs officer mistook the AK for an underwater spear gun (illegal in the Seychelles) and said he would have to confiscate it, but that he would give him a receipt for it so that he could pick it up when he left. They really are an innocent lot these Seychellois. When he tried to take it, a noisy wrestling match followed, a tug-o-war over the AK. The commotion caught the attention of a security officer, who picked up a telephone (it turned out he was alerting the military barracks) and then things got out of control, a loose round was fired from the AK and with that the security guard high-tailed it.

That was the shot I had heard when the woman had screamed. Next, we saw that one of the main party was down. Tragically, Johan Fritz, already some distance from the tussle, away in the arrivals hall, had been struck in the heart by the stray bullet and his life ebbed away in no time, right there, with nothing anyone could do to help him.

The fat was now in the fire. Gerry Puren, an older fellow from Durban who had been a pilot in the Congo and was a friend of Colonel Hoare, was on the roof of one of the buses, flinging down the bags and screaming at the guys to assemble their weapons. Then the Colonel said to me, 'Aubrey get the rest of your guys together, hotfoot it to Pointe Larue and delay any troops from leaving the barracks.' (Then followed the events described in the opening of this account.)

That was the last I saw of the engagement at the airport. I rely on the account of others, including Colonel Hoare, to sketch what happened next.

Our people sent another group to attack the barracks but an armoured car, which was blocking the gateway, turned them back. The whole force then threw a strong defensive position round the airport and somebody took the control tower without any problem. (Apparently the air traffic controller took refuge in a dustbin.) Meanwhile, a large number of civilians were herded into a hall for their own safety. Tanzanian troops made an attempt on the airport and three truckloads of Tanzanian troops came along the runway then advanced on foot, but ran away when they were fired on and were never seen again. However, one truck was left abandoned, a hazard to any aircraft that might want land. (I do not think the vehicle was left on purpose.) Two armoured cars then moved on the airport (it was dark by now) and shelled the buildings; one armoured car was knocked out by our men and the other retreated. All the while mortars were being lobbed at the airport, but not very accurately. We had lost the element of surprise but, as Colonel Hoare maintains in his book, there was no reason at all why we should not have been able to have taken the barracks at daybreak and completed our mission.

All the same, things had become badly unstuck. There was an attempt to get the Air Swazi crew to come back to the airport from the Reef Hotel, where they had already booked in, to fly the party out again. Jerry Puren went across the road outside the airport to a small petrol station and telephoned them. But when they heard what was going on they were dead off it, and I cannot say I blame them. In the end, their aircraft got hit in some shelling, which came from a distance, and got severely damaged. Then, as I am told, it became apparent that an Air India Boeing 707 was approaching Mahé to land. There is great dispute as to what happened next. Colonel Hoare says he ordered the former Rhodesian helicopter pilot who had taken up the air traffic control function to order the airliner to abort landing and head elsewhere – but a subordinate countermanded the order. The Natal Supreme Court found differently in the hijacking trial that eventually followed. I am inclined to believe the Colonel because the position was indeed by no means hopeless, according to the fellows I have spoken to. The Tanzanians had no fight in them at all. Our chaps could have taken the barracks, I am sure. But I do not intend arguing about it. Nor do I intend discussing whether or not Colonel Hoare was overruled by his men in the decision to board the Air India flight and leave the island. I was not at the airport: I was in the bush somewhere, bleeding badly. What matters to my story is that the Colonel and the rest of the party boarded the aircraft and took off for Durban, leaving Barney, me and a couple of others, stranded on the island. I blame nobody. We were casualties of war. We knew the risks from the start. But as I lay up there in the bush, wounded, and heard the Boeing take off in the dark, I did not know the others were on it. I did not realise yet quite how desperate the position was for me and others left on the island.

ARRIVAL OF THE MAIN PARTY 37

The main party disembarking from the aircraft

The main party's arrival

6
On the Hill and the Arrest

This now brings us back to where I was lying up in that little cave on the hillside, not knowing how close I actually was to Barney, who had come back to look for me. My leg was numb with pain; I had to drag it. When I crawled into the cave I could hear water, and as dawn began to break I saw there was a nice little stream running close by. But then, as it got lighter, I saw houses not very far from where I had laid low for the night. The stream was flowing down towards a little dam, from where I could see a pipe that led away from the dam towards another smaller group of houses. There were also footprints all about the place. This spot was going to be very unsafe.

I drank some water, washed a bit and tried to clean my wound. Then I filled my orange juice bottle with water and sort of staggered and crawled away, moving about fifty or sixty meters up the hillside. There I found another bit of cover, more like two rocks leaning against each other. I crawled in. Inside was a hornets' nest – they did not come out at me but I had to be damned careful – and the place stank of dog shit. But it might as well have been the Savoy. I did not stir until after eleven o'clock. I could see all the way down the hillside and not much seemed to be moving, but there was still sporadic firing between the barracks and the airport it seemed. I decided to get up the hill to get a better view. This was a nightmare – the pain, the weakness and dizziness – but eventually I got to the top and looked down from a small clearing. At this stage I was convinced our blokes had won. The firing had died down and I presumed the few shots I heard were mopping up operations. If I just sat tight, the group would eventually find me. I did not relish the idea of getting down that hill again with my leg. But then, as I looked, I got a nasty shock. An armoured car was still in the road outside the airport. Two Seychellois were in the turret, no mistaking that. Just then they loosed a shell into the airport building; there was an absolutely deafening crash as it struck, causing clouds of smoke and sending debris flying. It seemed things were not over, not by a long chalk (I was to later find out that they were firing on a completely empty air terminal). Just then a light aircraft flew overhead, then another. Spotter planes and they seemed to be searching the hillside. This did not look good at all. I got back to my little shelter as fast as I could, and next thing the bush was just full of Tanzanian soldiers, tramping about aimlessly and just firing shots at random into the underbrush. Terrifying stuff, they seemed to be shooting at anything that moved – chickens, dogs, pigs or whatever – and sometimes they came so close I could have reached out from my cave and grabbed one by the leg. But then I would have gone the way of the chickens.

I just sat tight, hardly daring to breathe. This was what one might call a tight spot. I did not really feel despondent about the expedition going wrong. I did not even think about it. When it is like that you shut out everything but the immediate danger. The seconds were ticking away slowly, very slowly. I began to think about what to do next. I had to hide until dark. Then maybe I could get down the hillside, somehow get into a pair of long trousers, make it to the Reef Hotel, and then get hold of one of the people I had met on the island, and they could arrange some medical treatment. I would then be in a far better position to make contact with the underground movement. After that, what? Maybe I could somehow get into a boat and slip away. Getting an aircraft was out of the question, as they would pick me up in two seconds. Maybe I would have to come back up the hill again. There was no obvious way out. Quite a while later, I pondered about my position; my first thoughts of what would happen if I was captured. I knew that the Tanzanians would be ruthless, also I knew that if captured, there would no doubt be interrogation to follow and I did not relish the visions I was having. I toyed with the idea of saving a bullet for myself if capture was imminent. It was then, that I knew life is too precious to take your own. I still do not know if it is a brave, cowardly or sad mental state, which drives someone to this extreme measure. I quickly put this idea out of my mind and focused on the task at hand – self-preservation. I sat tight for a few hours, a very long few hours. It took forever for the sun to go down and it took even longer for the darkness to fall, finally providing some form of cover.

Eventually, it was time and I set off into the dusk, a little before full darkness; I did not fancy doing that hill in the dark with my leg. I was taking a chance; this much I knew. There was a rough track winding round that part of the hill, and suddenly I heard the sound of a vehicle with a broken exhaust. I will never forget that, for at that moment a little girl in a yellow dress appeared on the path; she was waving for me to run and hide, all the while the sound of the exhaust got louder and louder. Almost in a flash, a squad of soldiers were piling out of this little truck type thing, yelling their heads off and shooting wildly. The Tanzanian soldiers had no allegiance to anyone, so they were firing indiscriminately at anything that moved, be they animals or civilians. Then there was a big explosion – I think one of them threw a grenade. I managed to get a move on, hobbling down the hillside somehow, heading for a little house on stilts. But before I could get there, the house just disappeared in a huge explosion that knocked me back and covered me with dust and dirt. I do not know if they took it out with an RPG or if it was another hand-thrown grenade but – kaboom! Suddenly that house was history; nothing left of it. (It later turned out nobody was in it, so nobody was hurt – but I do not believe the soldiers knew it at the time.) There was a strong smell of cordite and I was pretty dazed. It was getting properly dark now. I put my rifle across my chest and crashed backwards through the bush into a gully. Then I saw five or six of them coming up a path toward me. I just dived into the undergrowth and lay there. They were firing everywhere, making a terrible din. Bullets were ricocheting all over; it was an absolute nightmare. One guy was standing only about eight or twelve feet from my head and firing into the brush ahead of him. I could almost smell the fear in him as he fired burst after burst from above my head. How they did not get me God only knows. They seemed to sweep the whole area with automatic fire. Then they were gone – no searching for bodies or anything like that. I remember thinking that they were not very professional, thankfully. They were very jumpy and sent off rounds at every noise or slight movement in the undergrowth. On reflection, I am not so sure that they even knew I was in the vicinity and most certainly no one had pointed me out to them.

I lay there until it was pitch dark. By now a curfew had been imposed so there was little or no movement and no lighting. Then I got up and made my way down about 150 yards to another little house, a tin shack. I came up to the door and knocked. The door opened and I could see by the light of a little candle that a young Seychellois was inside with his wife and a little girl of about four. They just stared at me, absolutely startled. 'Look', I said to them, 'I'm not here to hurt you. I've come to help overthrow your government. I need some clothes. I've got a watch that I'll give you for a shirt and a pair of trousers.' They seemed to understand English.

The fellow went into a confab with his wife. They were talking in Creole and they did not seem to be hostile or animated in their gestures, so I was not too worried when eventually he turned to me and said, 'Yes, we'll do it.'

At that, relief flooded over me. I put my rifle on the table and then sat down in a chair to take a look at my wound. It is amazing how tiredness can cancel out all your alertness, all your training. Suddenly as quick as a flash he snatched my weapon from the table and pointed it at me; it was quite obvious that he had never used a firearm before, as he was shaking badly. What a sucker I was! I knew it was off safe and had a round in the breech. If he pulled the trigger, I would be gone. He started yelling to his neighbours for help, getting quite hysterical. He was very nervous and he bumped the table as he moved for the door. The candle fell over and set light to the newspaper they had spread as a tablecloth. The little girl ran for the door as well, and at this point I did something that still bothers my conscience today. I grabbed her and held her between the AK and myself. It was an impulse; I suppose you will do anything for survival, so I bargained with him.

'You get me the police and I'll put your little girl down. I've got a son the same age as your daughter and I don't want her hurt, the same way I don't want my son not to have a father. You get the police and I'll put her down. I'm willing to be arrested.'

Meanwhile, a whole crowd of neighbours had gathered in a half-circle round the door, shouting things like 'Terrorist! Bandit! Terrorist!' Some had axe handles, one had a mean piece of pipe and there was one guy practically foaming at the mouth, yelling 'Shoot! Shoot! Kill! Kill!' Then he pulled the rifle away from my captor, and at that point the magazine fell out.

The guy with the rifle tried to put the magazine back in the wrong way; he clearly did not have a clue either. But there was still that round up the spout and the way they were behaving it could go off any time. This was quite a predicament. I stood there in the doorway in the semi-darkness with only the odd flash of torchlight. The few faces I could see were mostly a mixture of nervousness; however, the most vocal of the men had a look of pure hatred. I am sure that he would have loved nothing more than to empty my magazine on me, there and then. By now the flames were throwing shadows on the walls and the whole situation had become very eerie and surreal. The chap who had initially grabbed my weapon at the house agreed to call the police and with that I put down his little girl. I was already feeling a bit ashamed. I then stamped out what remained of the flames on the table and newspaper.

'How far is the police station?' I asked.

'Close,' he replied.

'Let's walk then,' I said, momentarily forgetting about the pain in my leg. I wanted to get away from the lynch mob.

Also, I wanted to speak to somebody in authority. I planned to stick to my cover that I had come to the islands with Ken Dalgliesh to look at his chances of buying a hotel, and that I had got mixed up in all the nonsense at the airport purely by chance and had picked up the rifle just to defend myself in the confusion. It was a pretty slim hope, admittedly, but about all I had. We set off. I was making very heavy going of it in the dark with my leg. Then we saw little flickers of light in the blackness of the night; they were threading their way up the hill towards us. These turned out to be torches and before long three Seychelles police were with us, two women and a man. A feeling of relief ran over me. The man put his arm round me and helped me down the hillside to where they had parked their vehicle. (His name later turned out to be Harry and we ended up great pals and fishing mates – but that belongs to later.) They quickly handcuffed me and put me in the van and then we were off to the police station at Anse Aux Pins; this was a dingy little place lit with paraffin lamps. But they had been pretty kind and I was glad I had fallen into the hands of the police, not the army. Yet there were limits to the kindness. They had put me in a bare little cell and one of the policewomen was just passing me a mug of water when one of the men knocked it out of her hand and said, 'You give that man nothing!'

I had hardly had time to think much about how bad my situation was, when suddenly it got a lot worse. I heard a gearbox whining as a vehicle approached outside. I was to hear the same vehicle and the same whine many times in the months to come. There was a loud bang as the door violently burst open and in an instant a group of soldiers quickly filled the small space of the police station. There was a lot of shouting and gesticulating. Even though we were almost in the dark, as the police station was lit only by a couple of lamps, it did not stop them getting to grips with me. I got a thorough going-over: they handcuffed, hog-tied, and hit me all over with rifle butts. The lady police officer pointed out my gunshot wound, thinking they would go a little easier on me; this seemed to trigger off a more violent side in the new arrivals, as they really went to town on me, placing a rifle barrel into the wound, twisting it as they did so. They continued to kick me with heavy boots and hit me with their rifle butts. I was then dragged outside to be driven away to Pointe Larue barracks, the same place we had attacked the previous day. It was a confused sort of scuffle in the dark, lots of pain, blood pouring from my nose and mouth, and the wound on my leg starting to bleed badly again. They then flung me into that Unimog like a sack of potatoes. As we bounced painfully over the potholes, I knew the hard part had yet to begin.

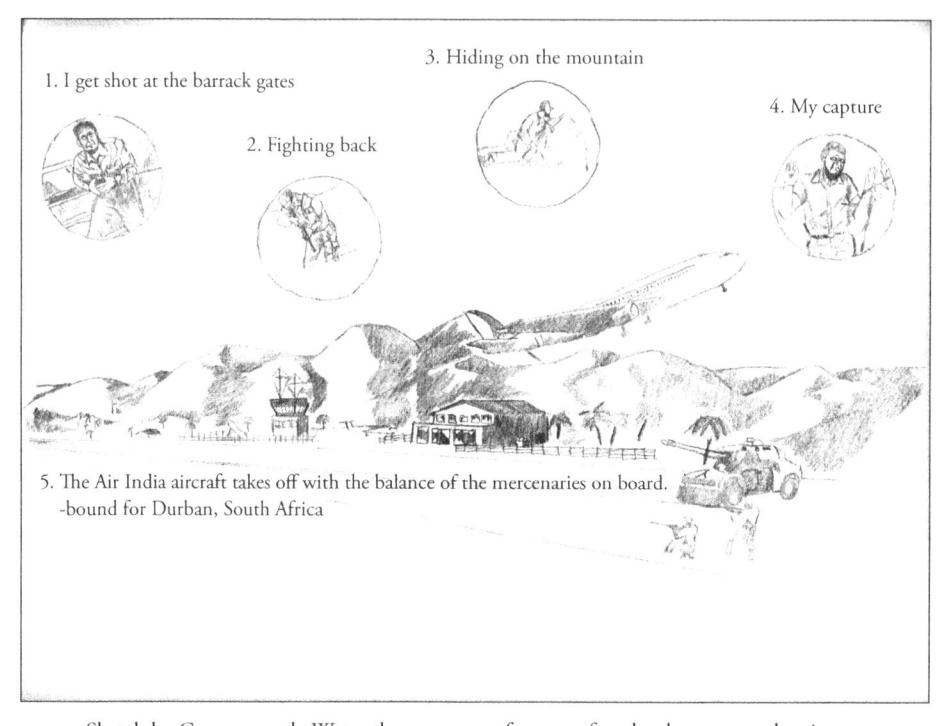

Sketch by Cuwan van de Wat—the sequence of events after the shootout at the airport

7
The Capture and Beatings

The next almost six weeks at Pointe Larue were like a mist of pain and blood; I was coming and going in and out of consciousness. It started when they hauled me out of the Unimog and gave me a going-over with boots and rifle butts, while they dragged me to the cells. I was handcuffed and hog-tied. (They only removed the hog-tie in order to move me around). There was nothing I could do to defend myself and I was staggering about with my leg wound. They stripped me of my clothing, and threatened to cut off my testicles, and to take my eyes out. By the end of that first night they had also broken my nose and this had made breathing quite difficult, although later when they left me alone in my cell, I was able to reset it with my hands, even though I was handcuffed. I was to reset my nose at least three or four times over the next few days. The people beating me were Tanzanian soldiers mainly. One sergeant I will never forget. He was a thickset, sadistic bastard with a face like a gorilla. He laid into me with his rifle butt, one in the ribs, then one in the face and then one in the balls; a few times he placed the gun muzzle into the wound in my thigh and twirled it around. It seemed he would never leave off. I am sure he was trying to kill me and I think it was only the Seychellois who called him off eventually. I was to see him in my cell almost every day for the next couple of weeks and always it was the same: he would give me the rifle butt.

'Fucking kaffir!' I would say, spitting blood through loose teeth.

It was all I could do, handcuffed as I was, and now I look back I can see it worked for me in a way. It got something off my chest and it did not make my beating any the worse because it turned out that 'kaffir' (unbeliever) is a word unknown to these East Africans. It is about the worst insult there is in southern Africa and it is a word I had always been brought up not to use, but in this situation I used it every time the bastard hit me and it gave me some satisfaction, without getting him stoked up even more. Other people whacked me as well, of course. Now and then a Seychellois soldier would run in with a klap, but as I say, that sergeant was the one who was really enjoying it and he had a face as mean as the devil.

I reckon I was half dead when they finally left me, still with the handcuffs on, in my cell that first night. I seemed to be bleeding from everywhere. It felt as if I also had a couple of broken ribs. My head was swimming, my ears were ringing, I had flashes of light before my eyes – even though the cell was in pitch darkness – and

I kept slipping in and out of consciousness. When I was awake, I ached all over. But the pain in my leg was just excruciating. I was sure that gangrene must have started by then, as the smell was terrible. The cell was no more than two metres by two and a half metres in size, more like a cupboard than any sort of room. It was also damp and had a terrible smell to it; this was to get worse over the days to come. There was no bed, no blankets, no toilet, and no water. Every time I asked for water they brought a tin mug full and poured it through the bars in the cell door; it then ran down the door onto the filthy floor. There was only the floor for calls of nature, disgusting, you can imagine. The cell was down a dark, unlit passage with no windows (as I was later to discover), which made it impossible to tell night from day. There were no lights; the idea was to cause disorientation as the beating continued – them shining torches in your face – as you would not know what day it was, what the time was or how much time had passed. There was one problem with this though: the soldiers had their radio in the guard room tuned into Radio Seychelles and this was blaring the whole time. By doing this they had lost a trick in the art of interrogation, as you knew exactly what day it was and the time of day. But it did not make the beatings any the less.

It seemed like about an hour or so after they left me collapsed there that I heard them bring Barney in. They were giving him the same going-over and I tried to call out some encouragement as they went scuffling past. My voice was no more than a croak and there was a din of stamping and shouting and swearing. But the odd thing is that when I spoke to him very much later, he said he heard me and took some heart from it.

Next day they brought in Roger England and Martin Dolinchek. The day after, it was little Bobby Sims, who had been staying in a safe house on the island. (It turned out they also had his fiancée, Susan Ingle, but she was never brought to the barracks or given the rough stuff.) They put Dolinchek in the cell next to me, and I will never forget what followed. There was a 'whack!' as someone gave him a flat hander, and next thing he shouted, 'I demand to see somebody in authority. I am not a mercenary. I am an agent of the South African government and I demand to see somebody in authority.'

It seemed to floor them as much as it floored me. There was a bit of a hanna hanna next door – no more flat handers – and somebody went hurrying away, obviously to call the person in authority that Dolinchek wanted. They soon hustled him out. I do not think he came back again to the barracks (Pointe Larue) and I did not see him again until we were in the military barracks at Unionvale.

For roughly the next few days they kept on beating Barney and me. I always hoped they would come to me first and get it over with, but often it was the other way round. They did not even interrogate us at that stage; it seemed they just wanted to beat us to a pulp to soften us up. The interrogation methods were not very efficient. But now came a new approach: they pulled a number of my toenails out with what I can only assume were a pair of pliers. This did not work at all, as I was in so much pain that it made no difference at all. In fact this only made me all the more angry. There were also a couple of surprise visitors in those first few days. On one occasion there was suddenly a Canadian pilot in my cell, giving me the sweet talk, telling me it would be better if I spilt the beans and got it over with. I knew he was a pilot, because he still had his flying kit on – he could have even been Biggles. I never did find out who he was, but he had also spoken to Barney. I assumed that he was something to do with the Tanzanians; he was probably the pilot that flew them to and from the island. A mercenary perhaps; the only difference was that he was on the other side? I did not trust him an inch and he got nothing out of me.

Then one morning a colonel called in on my cell. That did surprise me, not so much for his being there, but for his also telling me to spill the beans. He said that I should tell the Seychelles authorities everything I knew about the anti-government network on the islands. (Although I knew nothing about it anyway.) Why was he in with René's people? He had spoken first to Barney – had he been with Barney in the Congo with Colonel Hoare? – and when he spoke to me it was as if he knew me also from those days, but he was mistaken; I had never been in the Congo. He got nothing out of Barney or me. I was to later to find out that he headed up the Presidential Guard. The beatings went on daily, inflicting pain and humiliation. They were trying to break our spirit. Now our military training started to kick in.

Both Barney and I had stuck to the basics of our story from the beginning. This system normally works well when all of your team is trained to the same level. The secret of handling this type of interrogation is to stick as closely as you can to your original story and the most basic of truth. You should do this without divulging too much information, and then just hope that nobody else comes in with another story. If they do then you are literally on a hiding to nothing. Normally there comes a point where all information dries up and the need for continued beatings begins to diminish. This clearly was not the case here.

In the midst of the beatings two guards suddenly came into my cell and threw a bucket of water over me. This was not an unpleasant happening; it made a very welcome change from what by then had become the norm. I was quickly thrown some clothes and told to put them on. I looked enquiringly at the guard and then down at my handcuffs and finally at the binding on my legs; this simple gesture seemed to ignite something within the guard's brain as he burst into a tirade, kicked me a couple of times and then realised there was no way that I could magic myself into the clothing that was by now lying on the wet floor. He swore once more and stormed out. By now I was totally confused. As I began to gather my thoughts, the door flew open again. This time another guard who I had never seen before appeared and he was quickly joined by another two. The cell was now absolutely full, with no room for anyone to move. Expecting the worse I half waited for another series of beatings, but no, the newcomers had a bigger task at hand and that was to find a way of dressing me without undoing my bindings. I do not know how they achieved it, but a while later I was carried out and thrown into a canvas covered vehicle. I could hear more shouting coming from the cell area and suddenly another bundle was thrown on top of me. This I thought must be Barney but to my surprise, it turned out to be Roger England. What now? We were not allowed to even look at each other let alone speak and as we sped our way out of the barracks the mind began to wonder again. Is this the end of the road? We could not see where we were headed as we were made to lay flat on the floor with one of the guards standing on our chest.

When the vehicle came to an abrupt halt and the flaps were opened, we could see that we had been taken to the main police station in Victoria (this we knew well from our reconnaissance) and here we were told to not say anything or to ask any questions. What was this all about? We were then paraded, still badly beaten up, handcuffed, and myself limping badly, before the world press, in a small courtyard. It was difficult for me to take it all in. Cameras flashed and TV lights beamed on us. I had no idea who they all were. Though there seemed to be quite a crowd. They were not allowed to question us, nor were we allowed to speak to them. Then, as quickly as it all started, the freak show was over and we were hustled away, back to our hell hole in Pointe Larue.

But I took heart from this incident. I saw it as a turning point, because the world knew about us; we were on record and we were alive, even if we were if not so well. Now we could hardly just disappear. Until we had been paraded before those press people, I had a feeling the Seychellois could have just put us against the wall and shot us – the way the Tanzanians nearly did – and nobody would have been the wiser. Now it could not happen. Also, I knew Di would have seen me on television and would know I was at least alive. I knew she would be worried sick about my condition and my prospects. But while there is life, there will always be hope. I felt lifted.

On the morning of the 4 December, things began to change. Instead of a beating, a doctor was in my cell, probing at my leg wound and shaking his head. He gave his name as Dr Zech, although I am sure this was not his correct name.

'Would you like to go into hospital?' he asked. 'You could do with it.'

Like? In preference to this hellhole, no question. A few minutes later a pair of shorts and a shirt were thrown into my cell. (Though it was almost impossible to dress myself whilst handcuffed and in a lot of pain.) All of a sudden both Barney and I got hustled out to the Unimog. Once again we were laid flat on the floor of the vehicle, the flaps were tied down and we were whisked away at speed to the main hospital in the capital Victoria. It was a modern hospital, which looked very colonial and very clean. They then attempted to frogmarch us in, still handcuffed, very beaten up and not in good shape at all. This did not do my leg any favours. Once we were inside it was suddenly like a different world: sunshine, the smell of flowers and plants, everything neat and clean, doctors, nurses and orderlies in white uniforms. They were looking at us with real concern; they were not unfriendly at all. On the ground floor we were examined by a medic named Dr Desmond Fossbury; he was quite a tall, slender man who wore a ponytail in his hair, a kind and gentle fellow who made you feel a lot better right away, and who later turned out to be one of the bravest men I have ever had the pleasure of meeting.

'You need X-rays,' he said. 'Also, we need to give you an anaesthetic before we clean up that wound.'

After the past two days, I had to pinch myself to believe it. Before long there was a Seychelloise nurse leaning over me like an angel ready to give me the pre-op jab.

'A pity it didn't work,' she whispered as the needle went in. So there were people on our side. But it was a little late to be of comfort.

They wheeled me into the operating theatre and the last thing I recall before going under from the anaesthetic was Dr Fossbury arguing with the Tanzanian guard – a horrible little short-arse, hideously ugly, with a cigarette permanently in this mouth. The topic of conversation was about whether they could take off the handcuffs and move me onto the operating table. Permission was denied so I had to be worked on whilst still manacled to the trolley. The last thing I saw before going under the anaesthetic was this Tanzanian soldier in combat uniform wearing a doctor's gown and theatre mask, complete with a cigarette, sun glasses and, holding an AK 47 rifle. With that, the lights above the operating table began to spin and I was off to another world.

I came to in a bed, in a small ward on the first floor, alongside Barney. Both of us were handcuffed to the iron bedsteads with our arms spread apart and our hands above our heads. But to be there, between clean sheets and relaxed was the most wonderful feeling, as we also knew we were not in for another beating; this was like heaven. The Tanzanian guards were also there, glaring at us as if daring us to make a run for it – which we could not, even if we wanted to – and if we spoke to them or each other we would get an AK barrel jabbed in the ribs. But the nurses were terrific. They would curtsey to us as they came on duty, and fuss about us, and this seemed only to rile the Tanzanians all the more.

In the evening of the 6 December, Barney and I got into one of the tightest spots we were ever to be in on the islands. Barney grew up in east Africa, so he spoke Swahili. Not only that, he had learned it properly at school. His mother had wanted him to study French but he said Swahili would be a lot more useful. He spoke it really well. Useful is hardly the word; it saved our lives. We had been in there a few days and it was a Saturday night. I do not know if the guards had been drinking or smoking something, but Barney suddenly overheard them planning to shoot us as we lay manacled to our beds. They were going to use four shots on each of us, and then fire a couple of shots into the floor to simulate warning shots, and then take off the handcuffs and say they had shot us trying to escape. They did not know Barney could speak Swahili. They were deadly serious. During this period they began clearing away any metal objects from our bedside tables. (This was just in case there were any ricochets.) Barney whispered to me what was going on, and I managed to get the attention of one of the nurses.

'Call Dr Fossbury,' I said. 'These guys are planning to shoot us.'

She was gone in a flash. Almost in an instant Dr Fossbury was there in the ward. He walked straight up to these armed Tanzanians and asked them what was going on. He then told them if they wanted to shoot the prisoners they would have to shoot him first. The guard commander arrived in the ward – I think Dr Fossbury had sent one of the nurses to call him – and Fossbury read the riot act to him: the prisoners were his responsibility and so on, at that point he also told them that he was taking care of their comrades in the ward below ours and there would be very heavy consequences if we came to any harm. Talk about guts! With that he sat at the end of my bed. The Tanzanians were furious but they backed down. Dr Fossbury sat there with us until three o'clock in the morning and only left when the guards were rotated. I owe my life to that doctor, and also to Barney's magnificent choice of syllabus at school. They talk about medical ethics and that kind of thing, but to me it was plain guts and simple decency. I was to meet several people in the next couple of years that would give me a new respect for human nature, and Dr Fossbury was the first.

I wish I could say this hospital episode meant the end of the beatings, but it was only an interlude. The very next night the Tanzanians kidnapped us from the ward while Fossbury and the others were occupied elsewhere. This was done before the wound to my leg could be sutured – the doctor had said that because it had become so badly infected, they had to let it breath for a few days before they could sew it up. Once again they threw us in the Unimog like sacks of potatoes and took us back to Pointe Larue, where we each got another beating. This was welcome home and now wait for round two.

The interrogations now started all over again. It seemed to be mainly the Seychellois Army officers who were doing the questioning now and the Tanzanians would occasionally dish out the rough stuff. It was like a nightmare that is not going to end. I stuck to my story that I had come out with Ken Dalgliesh, who wanted to buy a hotel in the Seychelles, blah, blah, blah, and Barney stuck to his story that he was here looking at tourism. We just gritted our teeth, spat out the blood and stuck to our story. There seemed little else we could do. But the beatings got more intense and the questioning seemed very close to the mark. We did not realise at first that Dolinchek had sung like a bloody canary when they brought him in and that by now they knew the whole story: Colonel Hoare, the coup plan, the lot. (It later turned out Dolinchek had also told them the Kenyan government was also in on the thing. This was a BOSS agent?) This Dolinchek man had got up my nose from the start. Now Barney and I (also to some extent Bobby) were getting a hiding for no reason, other than that we had stuck to our story, not knowing he had already blown the gaff. Added to that, we got an extra beating for saying we did not know him.

'What is your relationship with Martin Dolinchek?' I was asked.

'Never heard of him,' I replied quite truthfully because he had come in with a false passport in the name Anton Lubic, and that is how we had known him. Crunch! I took a rifle butt in the face.

'You lie! Tell me about your relationship with Martin Dolinchek.' So it went on and on.

Beating after beating and they never seemed to get tired of it. Then there were the mock executions. At the beginning you were never sure if this was the real thing or not. These came in the form of either attempting to drown you in a bucket of water (water treatment) or by placing a bag over your head and putting a pistol at your head; they would burst into your cell, put a hood over your head, shine a torch at your head (this was quite hairy in the darkness of the cell), cock a revolver and hold it to your temple. Then, 'click'! An empty chamber that time? You would wet yourself the first couple of times, but after a while you would wish they would do it for real and get things over with. On one occasion they tried a new tact with me and came with a softer approach. There was no beating beforehand, more of enquiry.

'Tell us do you know an Anton Lubic?' the officer asked quite politely.

'No,' I replied immediately in the negative.

'Are you sure that you do not know this man?' He asked once more.

'No I am sure,' I said again, and with that they left.

I felt sure that this was a sign that the beatings were coming to an end. I was still pondering this when – 'bang' – the cell door swung open and slammed against the wall with a loud thud. This sound was followed by another crash as a boot made contact with my face. The beatings were certainly back with a vengeance. They propped me up and thrust a sheet of paper in my face. I could not make out what was written on it. Everything was a blur, my head was swimming and the pain had returned in a flash.

They then read out the contents of the document; it was a sworn statement by Martin Dolinchek (alias Anton Lubic) giving a detailed account of when, where and how we met, times, places etc… At this point I began to wish that they would just get one of these executions right and get it over with. But this thought lasted only for a fleeting second. You also cling to life. You are weak, confused, disorientated and in constant pain. You keep flaking out. The memory of it is more like a confused, painful dream than a series of connected events. But you do have your moments of clarity when you think of your wife, children, family, friends and the things in life that are worthwhile, and then, you cling to life even more than ever, although at times everything seems hopeless. I think the human body is a lot tougher than we know. It can take a lot of punishment and still recover. I believe it also builds up some kind of resistance to pain. After a while you do not feel it in the same way that you did at first. Nature is kind. But I think to come through the kind of experience Barney and I did without being broken, you need a kind of mental toughness. Military training gives you that mental toughness. But I think it depends in the end on whether that mental state connects with a state of spiritual toughness. I cannot speak for Barney, but I know that while I was going through that hammering, I somewhere accepted that whether I survived and whether I would ever again see Di and the kids again, depended on my faith in God to see me through. I knew Our Lord had suffered pain and degradation much worse than this – and in total innocence, not like us – yet he had risen above it and was there to comfort and support all who suffered.

I was also prepared to die if that was God's will. On one occasion when they put the hood over my head, I believed that was it. I asked for our Lord's forgiveness. Then asked Him to please let my family know that I had not meant to bring further hardship upon them and that I loved them very much. The most amazing thing then happened. It was very strange; I just felt calm and was at peace, something I had not known for weeks. As I said the Lord's Prayer, I had an orange glow about me – this was real, but something not quite of this world. I had read often before of people having out-of-body experiences, encountering a purity and light that they find difficult to describe. Suddenly it was the same with me, peace, contentment and I was bathed in this orange glow. This time they could not frighten me, as they had lost their power to harm me. But the execution was another hoax. Suddenly I was back in the land of the living, in that stinking cell, and fighting to live another day and ultimately to get back to my wife and family. I think the spiritual part of our mental toughness sometimes gets a bit flabby. It takes an experience like this one to tone it up. From here on, for the rest of our incarceration I knew that someday, somehow I would be reunited with my family. It is strange too, that from that point on the frequency of our beatings started to diminish.

Looking back over that period I felt sorry for a man like Martin Dolinchek. I do not think he had that mental or spiritual toughness. I do not feel anger against him, even though he got us a lot of beatings that were not necessary. After all this time I bare no grudge. But, as I say, he did get up my nose right from the start and the odd thing is that through all the rest of our time on the islands, he was always the one I got sat next to in police vehicles and was handcuffed to in court and elsewhere. Dolinchek and I were like Siamese twins. Maybe the Seychellois were rubbing it in.

Letter from Dr Fossberry regarding Aubrey Brooks

Aubrey Brooks

This man was brought to Victoria Hospital and admitted under my care on the morning of 28/11/81 under military custody with his wrists tightly bound with cord. Examination revealed bruises of the body and around the right eye. There was a penetrating missile wound (bullet?) of the back of the right thigh through the muscle bellies which had been previously and inadequately incised prior to hospitalisation.

Circulation in both hands had been grossly impaired as a result of the application of too-tight binding at the wrists. Surgical debridement of the thigh wound was carried out under general anaesthesia on the same day.

While in hospital the patient suffered from diarrhoea and difficulty in passing urine, for which conditions treatment was administered. The circulatory problem in his hands was continually aggravated; however, by over tight manacling and at one stage both hands being weight partly suspended thereby. This while under continual heavily-armed guard.

The patient was taken from hospital care at noon on 30/11/81 under military escort despite being declared unfit for discharge.

D.G.W.Fossberry
FRCS (Eng.) Frsc (Edin.)

THE CAPTURE AND BEATINGS 51

Aubrey Brooks shortly after his capture

Aubrey Brooks and Roger England on show to the world press

52 DEATH ROW IN PARADISE

Aubrey Brooks and Roger England at a press showing

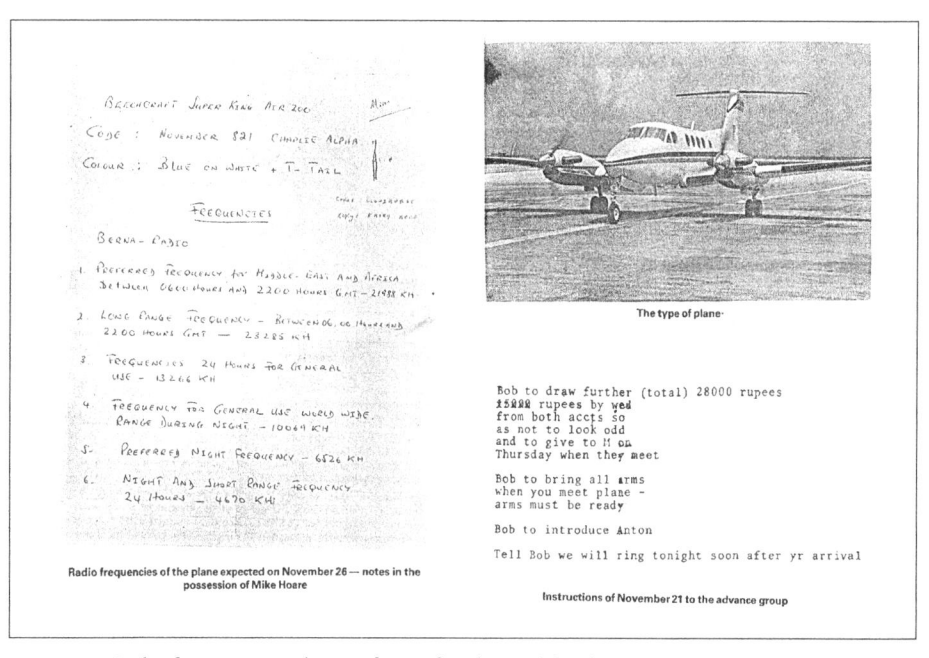

Radio frequencies and type of aircraft to be used for the incoming government

8
The Move from Pointe Larue Prison

A few days later we were taken out of the custody of the Tanzanians at Pointe Larue barracks. This was a major step for us. We were then taken to the military barracks at Unionvale, which was part of the headquarters of the Seychelles Army. Here, each of us was put in our own cell on the first floor; by our past standards, this was at least four stars. The cells were about five meters by four; here, we had a clean bed with a mattress, and a hand towel. The cells overlooked a courtyard to the front and behind us were pigpens and a chicken run. At Unionvale, we met up again with Dolinchek, who was in the cell next to me. We were to settle into a long and fairly uneventful routine of solitary confinement for the next nine months. This was only broken by being taken into town every couple of weeks to appear in court for remand. For these brief interludes we would be handcuffed in pairs and, as I have said, I always seemed to be handcuffed to Dolinchek. Sometimes when we appeared for remand, members of the public would taunt us – shouting 'Hey, Mercenaire!' etc. This only happened in the beginning, and mostly there was little or no hostility.

After Pointe Larue and the beatings, Unionvale was like a holiday camp. They gave us bread every morning for breakfast, and fish and rice for lunch and dinner. It never varied. The fish was not what you would call five star restaurant standard – bones, scales, often the fish's eyes as well – but it was fresh and good to eat. In fact the food was exactly what the soldiers themselves got every day, so we had no cause to complain. On Sundays we were sometimes given a boiled egg. It is amazing, when you are locked up, how important these little things become to you. You look forward to them for days in advance. Every morning one at a time, we were given a couple of minutes to do our ablutions downstairs in the toilets. This consisted of a cold water pipe that protruded from the wall, which was our shower and there was a single toilet; this area also doubled up as the washing area for the soldiers, plates of food etc. At night this place filled with enormous rats and also attracted hundreds of the biggest cockroaches I have ever seen. It is surprising how your body adjusts to that routine. On the first day of being allowed to use the toilet facilities, I remember the guard saying to me, 'If you want a piss, you can piss, if you want a shit, you can shit, if you want a shower, you can shower, you have two minutes, go.' What decisions! Such choices! And with only two minutes to complete all those tasks.

At Unionvale, for reasons I never quite fathomed, the lights were on in our cells twenty-four hours a day. It was the exact opposite to Pointe Larue, where we were in the pitch dark day and night. This was our lot for the time being, as we were still not allowed any reading matter for the first five months. After this period we were told we could have something to read; I was offered books on Che Guevara, the well-known revolutionary from Cuba and other similar books. I am sure that they had a fixation with military coups and the like. This was not for me, so I asked Major Marengo, who was in charge of the barracks, if I could have a bible, and eventually he got me a copy of the *Good News Bible*, plus the *Anglican Book of Common Prayer*. These I found to be a wonderful comfort. The Anglican prayer book sets out a special collect, or prayer, for every day of the year and it sets out specific readings from the Bible for every day. It meant I was able to join millions of people round the world in their daily prayers and Bible readings, and I really felt I was part of some vast network connecting to goodness and God. It lifts you. I grew up a Catholic and now I am non-denominational – in fact I accept all genuine religions, not just Christianity – but that phase of Anglican practice did a lot to keep me sane, and in good spirits, and to focus my thinking on what really matters in life.

After what we had gone through at Pointe Larue this was, as I say, a breeze. Barney and I came through the beatings pretty well. There is the pain and the physical damage, of course, but we stuck to our story. That is what you get from good training. You know that if you get captured you are going to get a going-over, and the trick is to stay fairly close to the truth, give away as little as possible, never compromising your own people. Little Bobby Sims did not have that training, which meant he got very confused and blabbed all kinds of stuff he need not have. For this he also got a few beatings more than he should have, simply because his story did not tie up with mine and Barney's. Dolinchek, as I have said previously, was a bit of a loose cannon in this respect, and the less said about him the better. If that was the calibre of the South African government's agents, no wonder they threw in the towel in the end. Dolinchek in the next cell was very scornful of my Bible reading and so forth. I pitied the man and I still do.

One day just before Christmas they came into my cell. It was early in the morning and as this was unusual. My first thoughts were what now? Fearing the worse, I was to be pleasantly surprised when they asked me to hold out my hands and they removed my handcuffs. It was the first time they had been taken off for nearly a month. By now I had nearly lost the use of my right hand from the over tight manacling. (A larger pair of handcuffs had to be obtained earlier on.) I then had to teach myself to use my left hand for the bulk of my tasks i.e. eating, toiletries, cleaning etc. But it did feel really good being able to lie down on a bed and sleep without having your body wrapped at some weird angle in order to get comfortable. It was a wonderful Christmas present, because from that day on the beatings stopped.

During this phase, I got to know more about the Seychellois and began to realise they were a gentle, good-natured people who meant nobody any harm. Also, I started to develop serious doubts about this story that the Seychelles had become an outpost for communism in the Indian Ocean, another Cuba. These folk were just too laid back and relaxed to be communists or anything else. I developed a great respect for Major Marengo in the various dealings I had with him at Unionvale and that I was also to have later. He was part of the military junta that governed the Seychelles and it turned out that on the last mock execution attempt on me at Pointe Larue (or was it a mock execution?), it was his voice that I heard telling them to take me back to my cell (as he had not been able to interrogate me, for he had been out of the country), so who knows, fate maybe! We also developed good relationships with the ordinary soldiers who were in charge of us. One such person was Sergeant Henry Victor, a huge, fat and jovial fellow who was the senior NCO. He was fascinated to learn that I was a qualified pilot – in fact three of us Barney, Roger and I all had our pilot's licenses. Meanwhile Jerry Puren had joined us at Unionvale. When he heard his name broadcast on the radio, he handed himself in. This he did in order to protect his relatives, who had been looking after him. He came up with a cock and bull story about how he had survived in the bush, eating coconuts and breadfruit. Yet he was immaculately turned out and clean-shaven. Some bush stay that had been. I fear that the Seychellois were a little gullible. Strangely enough, Jerry also had been in the Katangese Air Force during the Congo days; this is where he had met the Colonel.

On a number of occasions, I think when the Sergeant wanted some entertainment he would make his way to my cell and in a very loud voice say, 'Mister Aubrey, you a peelot?' (For this read Pilot.)

'Yes', I would reply, 'me peelot.'

Victor would hold his large belly and shake with laughter. 'Non, non, you not peelot. You mercenaire!' He found it very funny and he never tired of it.

To keep myself occupied, I composed three songs, 'Wherever I go' (that was for Di), 'My world, my window and me' (about my observations form my prison cell) and another song about life in general. I do not claim to be another Frank Sinatra but I can hold on to a note and it did not seem to upset the other prisoners. They were ballad-style numbers, something to keep me sane. Having no reading or writing material, I had to memorise both the verse and the chorus, whilst thinking about the lyrics (it certainly kept the brain active). Then one evening I heard somebody calling from outside.

'Mister Aubrey!' I went to the window; it was one of the guards looking up.

'Yes?' I replied.

'Mister Aubrey, please sing for me. You sing so beautiful, but please not the sad song.'

'What's your name?' I asked.

'Cleef.' He answered.

'Cleef? That's an unusual name.' I said.

'Cleefford.' (Clifford) was his rather curt reply.

'Okay, Cleef. Here goes.'

As I poured out my heart in song through that small prison window, I was aware how bizarre the scene was. Here I was serenading one of my jailers. But it provided a strange satisfaction as well, mingled with melancholy. After that I sang regularly for Cleef when he was on duty. In solitary you have to keep the brain active and I found a number of ways of doing this. Besides writing songs, I had noticed a number of patches on the concrete ceiling in my cell and while looking up at them I could make out a wide variety of shapes: a map of Africa, an eagle in flight, a yacht, etc. Over a period of time I had identified thirty different items and I would count them twice a day, morning and night; if I missed one I would start the count over again until I had found all thirty items.

After a few weeks the other fellows started getting mail from their families in South Africa. All the mail was intercepted and vetted by the military, of course. But I got nothing. It did not particularly worry me because I knew Di. She would not volunteer a single thing that might be sapped up, even distorted, and used in evidence against me. I had left for the Seychelles, with her informed only on a 'need to know' basis. She knew the operation was not in Zimbabwe, where I could be automatically charged with high treason and be sentenced to death. Beyond that, she did not want to know anything about it. She trusted my judgement on these kinds of matters.

***

On the 5 January we appeared in court for the first time. It was a very brief hearing and we were remanded; this process was to be repeated every two weeks. We had just got used to this routine, when unexpectedly, we were once again taken out of our cells and herded into a small room within the prison. It was in the middle of January and to our complete surprise, we were introduced to our council for the first time. You cannot even begin to believe what a tremendous feeling it was; we had not been forgotten and now at long last there was real hope. My joy was to be short lived, for when we asked our council Mike Hannon what our prospects were likely to be, he turned to me and said, 'I am afraid that you Aubrey will have to take the can for this one, if anyone is going to get the death sentence it will probably be you, particularly since you are the only one who was captured with your weapon and they already have a string of witnesses who said that you had shot at them.'

With that my heart stopped; here was my defence council telling me that I would be found guilty, long before the trial had even begun and worse of all, he was already preparing me for the maximum sentence – death. After that meeting we were taken back to our cells and what should have been a very positive afternoon for us all, turned into an absolute nightmare for me as I sat alone in my cell pondering what I had just been told. This was undoubtedly one of the lowest points of my life. Surely now I had no chance. It took days before I was to come to terms with what had been said. I then decided that all my life I had been a fighter and now was not the time to give up. Could I defend myself? What other options were there? I had to find a way, because I did not want that man to defend me. I just had to wait until I could get a message to Di or to the rest of our defence team.

A fortnight later we found ourselves once again at the courthouse in Victoria, for another of our fortnightly remands. After which we were taken to the main police station, in order to receive any mail that had been sent to us; the formality was that we would be taken out of our military vehicle lined up and wait for our name to be called. This too was another kind of experience, for this was the only time we got to physically see each other, and although we were forbidden to talk amongst ourselves, it is amazing how much communication you can have with just the use of your eyes. By now I was also used to not receiving any mail, although one does still keep hoping. So it was with great surprise that I was approached by James Pillay, Commissioner of Police, who had me un-handcuffed from Dolinchek and then led me to his office in the police headquarters. I was puzzled and once again the fear of the unknown took over. We would much later discover that the army thought that both Barney and I had still not told the truth, and that they were withholding our mail in order to get more information out of us or just for plain punishment.

'Frank I am worried about you,' James Pillay said to me (some of the Seychellois called me Aubrey, some Frank). He continued, 'Why haven't you been getting any mail? Don't your family love you?'

'Of course they do.' I replied. 'But they're not going to do anything that could compromise me or put me in anymore danger.'

He stared at me. 'Your wife must be worried sick. You have a wife?'

'Yes.' I replied.

'Do you have a telephone at home?' He asked. (In the Seychelles that is not an odd question, as private telephones are few and far between.)

'Yes, I do.' I once again replied.

He indicated to the telephone on his desk.

'That is one of two open lines on the island. Do you think she will be at home,' and before I could reply he said, 'Would you like to phone her?'

I could not believe my ears. My heart was pounding. Was this just another trick?

He then asked me my telephone number and the international code; I watched in almost disbelief as he dialled the number. As it started to ring, he handed me the phone, and suddenly, Di's voice was on the line. I cannot recall what we actually said. I told her I was with the Commissioner of Police and that all was OK, she must not worry. She said if there was a trial she would be there. It was very emotional and jumbled. Then I said goodbye and rang off. I did not want to abuse a privilege.

'Mr Commissioner,' I said. 'I can't thank you enough.'

'That's all right. I was getting worried about you,' he said as he got up and escorted me back to the group waiting in the courtyard.

My heart was pounding all the way back to Unionvale and worst of all, I could not tell anyone what had just happened, as any attempt to talk would have meant another beating from the guards or being reported on our return. The last thing I wanted to do now was get the Commissioner into trouble after what he had just done for me. That is what I call a great man. Yet we had come to the Seychelles to overthrow his government. What the hell was it all about? We were to have a lot of meetings with the Commissioner during our stay.

The months seemed to flow into each other with the same routine, court and remand, another two weeks, court and remand and so on. Then on the 5 February during what we thought was another remand, we were charged with treason; there was no big fuss made about it. The charges were read out and they informed us that the trial date would be set at a later date; it came as a surprise to us, but there was little or nothing we could do about it. When you are in a position like ours you are continually looking for any information that could have any bearing on your situation, no matter how small it is. In the middle of April we heard news that President René had made an appeal to the South African government for the death sentences on three ANC (African National Congress) militants to be lifted. They were Mcnibithi Lubisi, Petrus Mashigo and Napthali Manana. This came at the same time our trial date was announced as the 16 June. Could this be the bargaining ploy that we had been waiting for? Then nothing, everything went quiet once again. Then on the 24 May we were told that Mike Hannon was to be replaced as our defence attorney by Nicholas Fairburn. We did not know much about our new council, but I in particular found this to be good news.

Commissioner of Police James Pillay

THE MOVE FROM POINTE LARUE PRISON 59

The first remand

Going to court for one of the many remand hearings

Aubrey Brooks and Barney Carey

The last time we appear in court with Susan Ingle

9
The Trial

I had spoken to Di, which had lifted me, even though I was in a hopeless predicament. I was to see her again in the coming weeks when *Rapport* (the Afrikaans Sunday newspaper), who had secured her story, arranged for her to be flown to the islands and put into a hotel for the duration of the trial. The 100-year-old courthouse in Victoria was thought to be too small to accommodate the trial, as they were expecting a large contingent of international press and of course the official observers from a number of countries. This meant that a special dock for the prisoners had to be built and other alterations had to be made to the Peoples' Assembly Building, the Maison du Peuple (the Seychelles House of Parliament). They had planned correctly, as the world press were there, along with a fair number of observers who also attended, with representatives coming from Britain, America, Tanzania, China, Russia, and the Organisation of African Unity. This created a surreal atmosphere in which the trial would take place.

The 16 June dawned; this was the day that our trial was to begin. On our arrival at the courthouse we were taken out of the military troop carrier that had transported us on the short journey from the Unionvale barracks, amidst a show of force. We were handcuffed in pairs and I was cuffed to Martin Dolinchek; this always seemed to happen to my great annoyance. On that first day there were quite a number of inquisitive locals milling about outside. There were a couple of placards against mercenaries, but no real hostility that I could sense, more a buzzing of interest. One person who was there – and she turned up for every day of the trial – was a lady by the name of Jane Turner. She was the mother of the University of Natal academic, Dr Rick Turner, who had been gunned down in his home in Durban a year or two earlier. Turner had been a left-wing activist and was subject to a banning order by the South African government when he died. Nobody had been arrested for this crime – no great surprise when you consider the anti-communist sentiment at the time – and many people thought the security forces were responsible. Mrs Turner was convinced that Dolinchek was the culprit, as he had been responsible for keeping tabs on her son, and as far as I know she still believes that. We were led into the courtroom and each of us in turn was handcuffed to the railing that ran along the dock. This was very much for show, for the benefit of the international press and the public gallery. Out of the public eye during tea breaks and consultations with our legal team in an adjoining room, everything was much more relaxed.

Once in the courtroom, in front of us and to our far left was our defence team: Graham Fowlis, a Durban attorney; his assistant Jeremy Ridl; Kieran Shah, a Seychellois attorney; and Nicholas Fairbairn QC, a Scottish Barrister – a very colourful character who had handled a number of high profile cases. He was the Solicitor General of Scotland, a Conservative member of Parliament and he looked like someone from The Pickwick Papers. He wore the traditional black gown, fob watch complete with chain, the barrister's white wig and a pair of gold rimless spectacles sat perched on his nose. On our immediate left was the prosecution team: the Seychelles Attorney General Bernard Rasool; the Mauritian Attorney General; and four assistants; they were seated amongst a mountain of books, papers and legal literature. This setting was brought to order by a loud knock of the gavel heralding the arrival of Mr Justice Earl Seaton (the Seychelles Chief Justice). This was something that I was not prepared for, as it seemed to add another dimension to this already unbelievable setting, for he was a rather large black man who was born in the West Indies and educated in Britain. He was dressed in a scarlet robe and wore a full white judge's wig. He spoke with a very pleasing Jamaican accent and everything about him seemed totally surreal. It sort of took your breath away; it was so unexpected. This was like going to the pantomime. The only difference was that you were one of the performers and the stakes were high; you were going to perform for your life. The judge's bench was to our right and once the proceedings started it was like watching a tennis match, with the ball going from left to right and back again over the net.

Then I spotted Di. It takes a bit of adjusting to get used to any new surroundings when you have been in solitary confinement for a long time. But there she was opposite and above us, seated in the public gallery on the mezzanine floor; she was sitting with a policewoman at her side. My heart skipped a beat. She was sitting there staring at me, very calmly. The calmness seemed to reach out to me. I found it difficult to believe that it was her. She had lost so much weight and was looking really beautiful. She was very composed and this was of great comfort to not only me, but also for the rest of the guys. It gave us all a boost when we needed it most.

There was argument between our team and the prosecution over what the charges should be. The main count on the charge sheet was high treason, which automatically carried the death penalty. But none of us were citizens of the Seychelles. How could we be guilty of treason against a government that was not our own. There could be all kinds of other charges our lawyers argued – 'using force of arms' or 'attempting to overthrow a lawful government' or something of that sort – but high treason should be a non-starter. None of us owed loyalty to the Seychelles government. Also – and I was to get the significance of this only later – the prosecution could have been on shaky ground without the high treason option, because Albert René's government had itself seized power by force of arms, on the 5 June 1977, while President Mancham was out of the country.

Fairbairn was absolutely brilliant. The prosecution's attempt to charge us with high treason was, he said, like charging a motorist with rape for parking on a double yellow line. A crime has been committed but not the crime of rape. The argument went backward and forward. But things were rigged against us from the start. Long before the trial had begun, each of us was interviewed in Mahé police station by a group of people – three men and two women, as I recall – who said they were from the International Red Cross. They asked us to tell them in strictest confidence what had happened, how the coup had been planned, who was behind it and so forth. They said the information was needed so that the Red Cross could develop a strategy to stop such things happening again in the future… blah, blah, blah. The information we gave would go no further, they assured us several times, and we would be regularly visited by the Red Cross to ensure that we were being well treated and not subject to torture – none of which ever happened. We spilled the beans or about seventy per cent of what we wanted them to know anyway – you always hold back a bit – and it turned out that all this information went directly to the prosecution to be used against us. I do not know if those people really were from the Red Cross. They sounded Swiss or German. It could be we were fooled, dazed and confused as this was after being held in solitary and beaten to a pulp, but ever since then I have always looked a bit askance at the Red Cross, which is an organisation I had always respected before. I would like to be proved wrong about my suspicions, but perhaps I will never know. Much later, at the start of our trial it turned out that these people had in fact been part of the United Nations Commission. The document they prepared became the 'Report of the Security Council Commission of Enquiry Established under Resolution 496 (1981)' and every word we had said had been printed in this document; it had been distributed long before our trial had begun. I often wonder does this sound like an impartial body that is supposed to uphold the freedom and rights in our world today. I think not. In passing it may be worthy to note that the World Red Cross also never came anywhere near us. My point is that things were being rigged against us. The Seychelles government needed a charge of high treason and the judge allowed it. That afternoon the court proceedings were adjourned for the day and as we were being led to the army vehicle outside, I looked up and suddenly Di was there in the crowd. She put out her hand to touch me, but a soldier pulled her away roughly and appeared to throw her to the ground. At this, something snapped inside me. That day thankfully, I was handcuffed to Barney and I had only one free hand, but I went for the soldier dragging Barney after me. A scuffle followed, and Barney quickly restrained me saying this would not look good in the world press. Thankfully at this point an army officer intervened and told the soldier to leave Di alone. With that Barney and I were bundled into the armoured personal carrier and quickly rushed back to Unionvale barracks. The first thing I did when I got back to my cell was to write a note to Major Marengo and apologise for the incident. Fortunately the television crews had missed it; otherwise it would have been broadcast around the world.

    The second day of the trial started off with a bang, the Seychellois wanted a plea bargain: Susan Ingle (Bobby Simms's partner) to be freed in exchange for us pleading guilty. There was a short adjournment and we went into a huddle with our legal people. This was the first we had heard of the offer. I am not sure our lawyers were too happy with it but we decided to accept. It amounted to Susan's life being spared, against us pleading guilty in a case where we had no chance anyway. I do not think the Seychelles government would have harmed Susan whatever happened (we were to learn they are just not like that), but the way we saw it, we could not afford to take a chance. So we agreed to plead guilty and speed up the whole thing to get it over with. This too probably helped us in the long run, as the press made big news of it. They dedicated it to the front page with a headline that read: 'Four mercenary heroes have risen from the debris of the bungled Seychelles coup, they are Bernard Carey, Aubrey Brooks, Roger England and Jeremiah Puren. They have sworn to sacrifice themselves to secure the release of one of their colleagues. One by one they were asked to plead guilty and face the death penalty if it meant that Susan Ingle could be released. All said, yes.' Later that afternoon the Attorney General made a short announcement that all charges against Susan had been withdrawn.

The next day in court Dolinchek suddenly announced from the dock that he no longer wanted the services of the defence team. He would conduct his own defence. This was a bombshell. It also meant the trial would now run on for days. Which it did, as he continued to spill the beans in fine detail about how he was an agent of the South African government with an observer role in the coup and that he was not a mercenary; how and why the whole thing was set up; how the radio station was to be seized; that troops were to be flown in from Kenya; and that James Mancham was to be re-installed as president. The international press were there, lapping it up. The story went all over the world. The Seychelles government were getting the publicity they craved for, being portrayed as innocent victims who had been attacked by proxies of the evil apartheid regime. It worked for them a lot better than our brief admissions of guilt would have. The government needed pleas of guilty, in exchange for Susan Ingle's life, and they got them. They wanted full details of the planning of the coup, and they got them via the 'Red Cross'. They also needed the widest international publicity possible, to strengthen their case for reparations and maybe international assistance, and they got that via Martin Dolinchek.

The trial was a blur: one day ran into another as we were transported between Unionvale and the courthouse; Dolinchek singing his story from the dock; cross-examination by our lawyers; and short recesses during which Di was allowed access to me. The days mingled with a lifting of spirits, and pain. What do you say to your wife who has stood by you through everything when you know you are going to get the chop; she knows, you know that she knows, and she knows that you know that she knows. It is too much; it is hopeless. After a couple of days, I was told that they had agreed for Di and me to meet at Unionvale barracks (the prison where we were being held). The meetings were to take place in the presence of Major Marengo, in his office; they took place mostly mid-afternoon. The first meeting was very difficult; there is so much you want to say, but you are sitting in front of the Prison Commander. (I think it was just as uncomfortable for him as well.) That first meeting lasted only twenty minutes and as the meeting came to an end there was so much left unsaid. However, we were both very grateful. The subsequent meetings lasted longer and longer, as we found ourselves sitting talking with the Major. Here too, was another big lesson in both our lives, as we came to realise that people of vastly different backgrounds and political persuasion, can agree to disagree and we suddenly found ourselves with a lot of common ground. I found a new respect for the Major, as our discussions developed; the conversation covered a wide range of topics, home décor, international politics, family, etc.

Over the next days, our legal team did the best job possible. It was a hopeless case from the start. We all knew what we had done and what we were in for. But there were the brighter moments. One morning Nicholas Fairbairn greeted us with enthusiasm as we arrived, thumbs tucked into his gown, his glasses flashing with excitement.

'Gentlemen, good news!' he beamed.

Good news? What kind of good news could he have? We looked on inquiringly.

'It's a boy!' he said in a rather triumphant voice.

A boy? What was the man on about? Had he flipped his lid? Was the trial taking its toll? It turned out he was talking about Princess Diana giving birth to Prince William. He was an ardent royalist (so am I for that matter) but he seemed not to realise, that being in jail and struggling for our lives on an obscure island in the Indian Ocean the way we were, the great event had passed us by. Fairbairn also held some sort of honorary post that involved inspecting Britain's lighthouses with Princess Margaret (I think they were the official Keepers of the Lighthouses on the British Isles), and he was able to tell us many amusing yarns. It did not help our case, but it was some sort of temporary escape.

It was during a recess on a Thursday, when Dolinchek had finished his evidence, that we asked Fairbairn what would happen next. He said the judge would probably adjourn the case until Monday so that he could deliberate for a couple of days. It was possible he might have judgment ready by then. Back in the dock, we were expecting a recess, but suddenly I was called on to the stand. Justice Earle Seaton asked if I had anything to say before sentence was passed. Even to me, who knew little about the law, this seemed to be rushing things a bit. Also, I had nothing prepared. I stood up and said, 'Yes, your Honour. I would like to apologise to all the people I may have hurt, intentionally or unintentionally. We didn't come to the island to cause pain and suffering and believed we were doing the right thing. So to anybody I may have hurt I apologise and I apologise to the people of the island and especially to my wife, family and friends.'

With that, I was about to sit down, fully expecting the rest of our guys to be questioned as well, when he continued with the verdict whilst reading from the charge sheet one item at a time. On charge one, importing weapons of war into the country: guilty. On charge two, waging war against the Seychelles: guilty. On charge three … I could hardly believe what I was hearing, when he suddenly said and on charge four, treason: I find you guilty. He then went on immediately to pronounce the death sentence saying, 'Aubrey Frank Vincent Brooks I sentence you to suffer death in the manner authorised by law…' It is very ponderous. Even when they are killing you, it sounds like a lot of bureaucratic waffle. It was at that point I showed some good upbringing. In reply I said, 'Thank you, your honour,' and then sat down.

This had taken everyone in the courtroom by complete surprise, including the legal teams on both sides. I looked up at Di in the public gallery. The Seychelloise policewoman had her arm round her. Di stared at me. I looked her in the eye; there was a look of terror and disbelief – but a picture of strength and calmness. I will never forget it. The strength that she showed at that moment was absolutely amazing and this was of great comfort to all of us in this very dark time. This was an experience that I would not wish on anyone, not even my worst enemy. I then looked down in disbelief; it had happened so fast. I was overcome with a feeling of complete helplessness and wondered how Di would cope.

The others were sentenced. Jerry Purin, Roger England and Barney Carey also got the death sentence. Bobby Simms got ten years and Martin Dolinchek got twenty years.

At the end of the day's proceedings, Di had always been allowed access to me briefly. This time it did not happen. What do you do when you have received the death sentence? You carry on. I had already put my faith in God. The defence team were convinced we had an excellent chance on appeal. As I have explained, there were several features of this trial that made it more like a kangaroo court than anything else. Fairbairn and the others said the next step was to take an appeal to the International Court of Justice at The Hague, focusing among other things on the way we were convicted of high treason while we were not citizens of the country. In fact the four of us who were sentenced to death, became the first people in history to be found guilty of high treason as non-nationals. The only other person that was involved in a similar trial to ours was William Joyce, the man with the famous nickname 'Lord Haw-Haw', Britain's most well-known traitor, who broadcast for Germany during WWII. He was executed in the Victorian prison of Wandsworth on the 3 January 1946. To this day, because we dropped our appeal and our case had not been heard in The Hague, we still remain unique in the history books.

We were not to realise at that stage that there were reasons the Seychelles government would not welcome going through the appeal process. There was the fact that they themselves were the result of a coup, which could have been argued in an international court, and also the publicity was beginning to turn counter-productive. Although it suited the government politically, it was hammering the Seychelles tourism industry, which had already lost billions through bad publicity. It would be better if the whole thing were to be quietly shelved for a while.

In the end, an appeal was never mounted. Other things were stirring, totally unpredictable, nothing at all to do with us and absolutely unknown to us, and these were to decisively affect our fortunes in the years ahead.

THE TRIAL 67

Diane Brooks on the first day of the trial

Martin Dolinchek and Aubrey Brooks leaving court.

Aubrey and Diane Brooks.

Martin Dolinchek and Aubrey Brooks on the way to court

THE TRIAL 69

Nicholas Fairburn Q.C.

Jeremy Ridl and Nicholas Fairburn at the Pirates Arms

SEYCHELLES   Cr. Side No. 4/82

In the Supreme Court of Seychelles

~~In the Magistrates Court~~

WARRANT OF COMMITMENT
(Section ~~224~~ of the Criminal Procedure Code)
266 (8)

~~To the Superintendent of Prisons~~ To Second Lieutenant Andre Ciseau

Whereas Aubrey Frank Vincent BROOKS

of Amanzimtoti, Natal, South Africa

was on this day convicted before this Court of the offence Treason

under Section 39 (1)(a) of the Penal Code

and was sentenced to suffer death in the manner authorised by law.

You are hereby required to receive the said Aubrey Frank Vincent BROOKS

into your custody in the said prison, together with this warrant. ~~and there carry the aforesaid~~

~~sentence into execution according to law.~~

Given under my hand and the seal of the Court this   6th   day of July   1982.

(Seal)   Chief Justice/~~Judge~~
                                      ~~Magistrates~~

The death warrant for Aubrey Brooks.

10

The Mutiny

As I have mentioned, at Unionvale barracks the lights in our cells were on twenty-four hours a day. So by now we were used to living in light 24/7 much like a gold fish in a bowl. It was very different to our earlier experience, where we were kept totally in the dark and beaten regularly. Then, at about 2100 hrs on the 17 August the lights suddenly went out. It was a bit unnerving. You are sitting there under sentence of death and suddenly there is a change in circumstances. It makes you nervous, and makes you wonder. Dolinchek straight away started aloud on how they were going to take us out to sea in their naval boat the *Topaz*, weight our bodies down, and then dump us in the Indian Ocean. The guy has a vivid imagination and he had no belief in anything, so he tends to get over the top very easily. At around midnight I heard a shot go off. This first startled me. Then I thought it was just another AD (an accidental discharge from one of the firearms – it was fairly common in those days) and I tried to get some sleep, but something unusual was going on. In the darkness of the barracks you could hear the shuffling around of the soldiers and their muffled voices. Sergeant Victor came past my cell and I asked him what was going on. He said, 'Don't worry, just relax.'

Then at first light a number of shots rang out. Shortly afterwards Cleef appeared at my cell window. I also asked him the same question. He said, 'You must not worry, everything she will be alright.'

That was the last time I ever saw him. We could now hear that the shouting was getting louder and people began running about. There was a real commotion and in the midst of this two more people were brought to the cellblock and locked up. We had no idea who they were or where in the block they had been placed.

Then, soon after daybreak, Sergeant Victor and a few armed soldiers came to our cells. They opened the doors then told us to hurry up and get our ablutions done. This too was a new experience, as we were in solitary confinement and were never allowed to be together, and with the urgency in his voice we all made a beeline for the toilet and shower. You can imagine the pandemonium as the six of us were trying to get cleaned up as well as trying to find out what was happening. We expected to be carted off somewhere, but instead we were herded back to our cells and given our usual breakfast. This was all done at the speed of light and before I knew it, I was back in my cell none the wiser as to our rather precarious position.

A while later Sergeant Victor came and broke the news to us: there was a mutiny. The non-commissioned officers wanted two majors sacked from the military junta (the junta was responsible for governing the Seychelles), apparently for giving their subordinates a very hard time. They had arrested a lieutenant and a sergeant major, who were in command at Unionvale, and locked them up. They had also seized the radio station next door (the same one I had been tasked to capture in order to play the tapes from) and from there they were now broadcasting their demands. Unless these were met their captives would be killed. I think booze and drugs also had a lot to do with this business, but that was the gist of it. They then asked us if we would join them in the mutiny. They said that they could do with our military skills and that they would release us and arm us if we agreed.

This put us in a bit of a spot. How successful was this mutiny likely to be? If we joined it and got captured again, our slim chances would really be zero. Yet here was freedom beckoning. We discussed it loudly, up and down the cells corridor. Until now we had been forbidden to communicate – guards were always around to stop it – but all that had disappeared. Our general position was that we would play it by ear. If the mutineers released us and gave us weapons we would play along with it but we would do whatever suited us best, including going over to the government side if that was the way things were moving. We played our cards close to our chest.

The set-up at Unionvale was that the cells had windows and these overlooked the courtyard in the centre of the barracks. I was looking down into the courtyard, my mind in a bit of a whirl at what was going on, when I saw the baker's van drive in. I had been watching him for months, as this had always given me something to do (although he never ever looked up at us). He arrived as usual and got out to offload the bread, but first had to look round for somebody to sign for it. Nothing was as normal, people were hurrying about, and nobody wanted to know about signing for bread. I could see he was getting a bit frustrated, probably threatening to take the bread back. But at last he managed to get a signature and started offloading.

Then all hell broke loose. Mortar bombs started raining down. You can imagine what that was like. Explosions, the buildings shaking, dust everywhere, screams and yells. Here this guy was offloading bread from the baker's van, right in the middle of it. Maybe he was deaf; he just carried on. But then a mortar landed close enough to him to let him know that he was in the wrong place. With that two soldiers rushed past him carrying one of their wounded comrades. He looked up somewhat dumbfounded and in absolute horror. Next thing he dived into the van. There was much crashing of gears and a large amount of wheel spin as he roared off, leaving a big cloud of dust in his wake. I was thinking how bizarre and really funny the scene before me had unfolded, when suddenly I could hear the whistle of another mortar bomb approaching. Bang! There was a loud thud and lots of debris was showered all over the place. I was brought back to reality as another motor bomb landed and this time it was very, very close to our cells. The loyal troops were now finding their range; the courtyard in front of us was the target (this is where the mutineers were directing their operations from).

The mortars just kept raining down. It was like being in the trenches in the First World War. Here was a turn-up. People offering to release us and arm us, yet here we were still locked in our cells and mortar bombs pounding the barracks. The cellblock seemed solid enough; however there was just an asbestos roof, wooden beams and a pine ceiling above Roger's cell – a motor bomb would have no problem with that and we were the centre of the target. The blasts were unnerving. I could hear the sound of the discharge as it was launched and I would count the seconds from the launch as it hurtled its way towards us, and then the short whistle before the blast as it landed. We were being fired on from somewhere up on a hill in the town above us. A dreadful new sound joined the yells and screams of the soldiers. There were chicken runs and pigpens just below our cells and to the rear of us. I could not see them but I had often heard the clucking and grunting. Now they were squawking and screaming. It was like a soundtrack from hell. I do not know if they had also taken a hit or were just terrified, but the noise was pretty bloodcurdling.

We were still locked up. The mutineers would come and promise us that we would soon be released, and we would soon have guns, but the truth is they were afraid to let us out. They were terrified of mercenaries. We had been built up into demons or supermen by all the propaganda, and the exploits of people like Bob Denard in the Comores were well known as well. They wanted us to help but they were afraid of what we might do if we were freed and given weapons. So we stayed put. It went on all day, and all night and the next day; between fifty and sixty mortar bombs rained down on us over that period. The bombs were shaking the building, accompanied by rifle shots, machinegun fire, pigs squealing, yells, and shouts. The hot humid air now also smelled different. Mingled with the thick dust, were the smells of cordite, explosives, spent cartridges, blood and other aromas. This added to the sounds coming from the livestock area had now made it a very unpleasant place to be. It was impossible to know what was going on. The ironic thing about this period is that with all the mortar bombs and bullets flying around, the only person to sustain an injury was Jerry; he had cut his knee whilst diving for cover under his bed at one of the first barrages of mortar fire.

The second night Roger England managed to force his way through his ceiling (he was being held in the old visiting area where the roofing was not quite so robust). The guards had abandoned us by now and he got out. He found the guardroom deserted, took the bunch of keys and let us out of our cells, also the lieutenant, sergeant major and a Creole named Jean Dingwell, who had been arrested as a member of James Mancham's resistance party. We were able to dress the wounds on the two men that we had released. (Barney had acquired some medication, bandages, dressings, along with a radio, during a short recce to the guard room.) It looked more likely that they had taken a beating rather than injuries from the attack. They thanked us, and then quietly slipped away. During this time Barney and Roger were able to get a message to army HQ via radio or telephone, that the men had been released and that numbers of soldiers in our barracks were diminishing. As it turned out the newly released officers linked up with the loyalist soldiers. We decided our safest bet was to lock ourselves in the kitchen and sit it out until things calmed down. Dingwell stayed with us. Dolinchek was always the odd man out. He found a Seychelles Army uniform hanging from a peg somewhere and put it on (all we prisoners had, was a pair of shorts); he then made his way out of the battle area and off up the hill. I believe he later made quite a song and dance about how he linked up with the loyalist army and proved his loyalty to the government, but if that is true it did not help him much. A couple of days later he was back with us as a prisoner.

Meanwhile, we settled in the kitchen for the duration; this was a great place to be, it was solid and we had a good supply of food and medication. We were now helping ourselves to a square meal for the first time in months. Also, we had a radio and we were receiving the mutineers' broadcasts. They had discovered that their hostages, the lieutenant and sergeant major, had escaped. Now it was the mercenaries who would be killed if their demands were not met. A lot of the broadcast was in Creole and quite a fair amount in good English. It was a strange feeling to sit there chowing and hear your name being read out for execution, by people who were in a radio station studio which was right next door to our barracks. We had only a roughly barricaded kitchen door which was keeping the mutineers from us.

But eventually things began to quieten down. I think the mutineers had enough of being mortared. I also think that this probably coincided with the booze and the drugs wearing off and the hangover setting in. It was quiet for a while, and then we could hear new sounds; people were stomping about the place with authority. The firing and mortaring had died away. There was a banging on the kitchen door. We assumed it was the loyal troops, and rather apprehensively, let them in and put our hands up. The loyalist troops had arrived. They had been alerted by our radio contact with a lady radio operator in the military, and the returning officers, who in turn informed them that the prison was now deserted.

The new group realised who we were, but they seemed a bit at a loss as to what they should do with us. It turned out that the mutineers who by now had surrendered – had been responsible for a firefight that had left a large number of soldiers on both sides either killed or wounded over the two days. They were now going to be placed in the cells recently occupied by us; they were to be crammed into the few cells that had been our home for so long. Eventually the five of us were put in the laundry; Martin was to join us later. In the confusion of the rebels being rounded up and placed in our cells, we took the gap and quickly sorted out the laundry. We found items like a broom, a small table, and the radio that we found in the guardroom had also became proud possessions of ours. By the time the officers returned to Unionvale prison, our new quarters were looking spotless and quite ship shape. Solitary confinement was a thing of the past. We could talk and plan. We could offer one another strength and comfort. It was a whole new phase.

But there was more to it than just that. Somehow I sensed that we might have reached some kind of turning point, as two loyal Seychellois – a lieutenant and a sergeant major – owed their lives to us. The destruction and bloodshed caused by the mutineers, and those sent to suppress them, was far greater than anything we had done. Our lawyers were working on an appeal to the International Court of Justice at The Hague. Our conduct during the mutiny could surely do our cause no harm.

Having a common cell turned out to be a mixed blessing. At least in solitary you are thrown back on your own reserves of strength and mental toughness. You cope on your own or you do not cope. In a common cell, all kinds of new forces come into play: petty jealousies and intrigues, and irritation with people whose company you cannot escape. There are squabbles over such things as food and chocolate parcels from the British High Commission (posted by the families) and over cigarettes (I do not smoke but cigarettes were a constant source of friction among some of the others). I do not want to ever again be in a prison cell, but if I had to be, I would rather be in solitary.

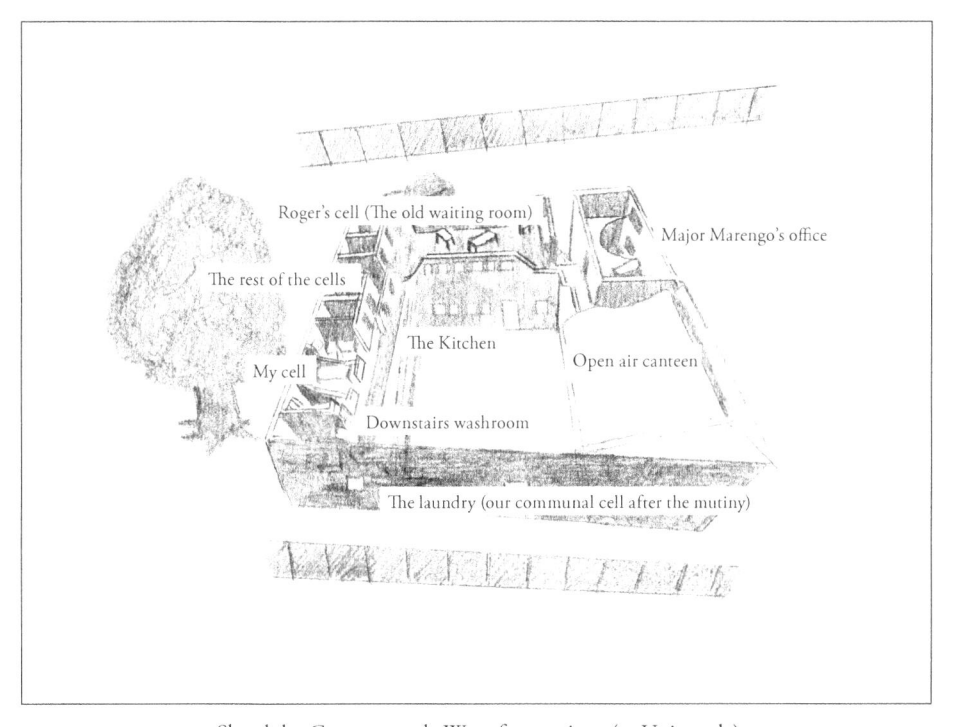

Sketch by Cuwan van de Wat of our prison (at Unionvale)

11

Meeting the President

It must have been five or six weeks after the mutiny when there was another sudden change in our prison routine. Quite late at night, Barney, Roger, Jerry and I were issued with clothes that had been taken from our hotels after our arrest – shirts, shorts and shoes – and told to put them on. Then the lights went off in our cells; a few minutes later the barracks was in darkness. It was pretty eerie. Were we about to face the firing squad? All kinds of thoughts flit through your mind. We were taken downstairs and told to get into a troop carrier that was parked in the courtyard. Guards got in with us. The canvas sides were fastened down. We could not see where we were going as the vehicle drove out of the barracks.

From our new quarters in the laundry, we looked out over the harbour and we had noticed the Seychelles' small naval craft, the *Topaz* – not much bigger than a launch – was back in commission after having had engine problems for a number of months. Roger in particular was convinced we were heading for the harbour; we would be taken on board, taken out to sea, shot and dumped overboard as shark meat. It went through all our minds, but I was not so sure. Would René do a thing like that with a large press corps still on the island, destroying the favourable publicity he had had at out trial? An appeal was about to be lodged at The Hague. It did not quite add up. Also, a puff of wind would shift the canvas flaps on the army truck every now and then, and we would get a glimpse of the street outside. We had done a very thorough recce of Victoria before the balloon went up and we were not headed for the harbour. The vehicle went past the police headquarters, which I think we all thought was our destination. It then moved higher up the hill as if we were heading for the presidential palace. Barney agreed with me as we conversed in whispers. The vehicle suddenly swung through a pair of large gates and down the driveway towards this big colonial style house. We then knew where we were. What now?

The vehicle came to a stop in the pitch dark. The only lights that were visible were the park lights of our troop carrier, pretty eerie. When we got out of the vehicle we were surprised to find that Major Marengo had got into the cab before we left Unionvale. As we stepped down from the vehicle into the musty, humid, blackness of the night, I looked around and as my eyes were getting used to the darkness I could make out the contours of the lawn. There seemed to be a lot of shrubbery around, except the shrubs were moving about; they turned out to be groups of soldiers. The place was heavily guarded. There was no moon and the only illumination was a shaft of light that came from a doorway on a colonial style veranda. As we walked towards the light the Major turned to us and I think he was talking to Gerry when he said, 'Be careful, in case you fall down.'

We were met by Max Fontyn, the Deputy Commissioner of Police. Little did I know at that time, but I had inadvertently caused him to be held under house arrest for a few days soon after our capture. This was because during my interrogation I had named Max as the person who had been in charge of the operation. (This was a name that had just popped into my head from the movie *Mad Max*. I had done this in order to not name Colonel Hoare.)

The authorities had at first thought that he was involved in the coup attempt and only a while later had a lifted his house arrest. However, he now guided us up on to the veranda and through the door into an entrance hall. He tapped at another door, put his head round and then gestured for us to come in.

Standing behind a desk was a short, stocky man with wavy dark hair and ruggedly handsome features. He gestured for us to sit down at four chairs placed on the opposite side of the desk. This was President Albert René. Fontyn looked for a chair for himself, but René said there was no need for him to stay. Fontyn looked uncertain – you do not leave your president unattended with four dangerous mercenaries – and then, very unhappily he left.

René spoke, 'Good evening, gentlemen. I take it that you know who I am. I'm the man you came to kill.'

This was pretty direct. I think we all winced a bit. None of us had come to the islands to be part of a firing squad, and Colonel Hoare had told Mancham's man Hoareau that we would not be part of any political reprisals. But you have to be honest. There is no knowing what the Seychellois themselves might have done if we had succeeded, or the Kenyan troops who were supposed to be flown in afterwards. Then he turned to me and said, 'You're Frank Brooks?' (The Seychellois often called me by my second name instead of Aubrey; I am not sure why.)

'Yes Sir' I replied, thinking the worst.

He continued, 'I would just like to say your wife has been a credit to you, to all of you, the way she has conducted herself on the island. The way she has handled the press and befriended the people of the island has been noted.'

We relaxed a little at that. This was not going to be something sinister, it seemed. But it struck me: this was the president talking to a bunch of mercenaries who had come to overthrow his government. Although he was small in stature he certainly had a big heart.

Then he asked us why we had come to the islands, how we had been recruited. By now there was no great secret about that. We said we believed we were fighting in the cause against world communism. He seemed a bit shocked at that.

'But I'm not a communist. I'm a socialist.' He quickly informed us.

We were none of us experts in this kind of thing. I had always believed a socialist and a communist were much the same thing. A socialist was a communist who sat on the fence and took help from both sides. But it seemed things were not as simple as that. René went on about how much his socialist government had done to uplift the people with schools, clinics and that kind of thing. It was really odd. Here we were, four men under the death sentence for trying to overthrow the government, having a civilised political discussion with the guy we had come to destroy.

Then René came to the point. Our attempted coup, and all the publicity that went with it, had done tremendous damage to the Seychelles tourism industry, he said. (I was to find out only later just how much damage. Arrivals had dropped by something like eighty per cent. The cash needed for René's social projects was just not coming in any more.) The trial and all the publicity had only made things worse. So too had the trial in Natal of the mercenaries who had escaped by the Air India jet to Durban. Both trials had received a lot of publicity around the world. Then he asked if we would consider abandoning our appeal to The Hague. He said that they did not need another trial, another round of negative publicity. He then went on to say that at a later stage, when the excitement had died down and the event had been forgotten, he could commute our sentences and eventually arrange an early release. It could not be done right now, but if we were taken out of the public eye for a time it could be arranged. Roger England asked the obvious question. If we dropped our appeal, what guarantee was there that the death sentences would not be simply carried out?

He replied, 'As long as I'm alive, I'll give you my word.'

At which point we said that we would be happy to dig foxholes in the garden in order to ensure that he was safe and that nothing would happen to him; to this, he just smiled and then continued. René also said he was disappointed at being unable to get a dialogue going with the South African government in order to do something about our case and arranging our release. He said it was obvious that Pretoria had backed the attempt, yet attempts to engage the South African government through diplomatic third parties had come to nothing. (I expect he was keen to get the South Africans to pay reparations for the damage.) I suggested getting our legal defence team to work on it and suggested that my wife Di could get it moving right away. With that he asked me if my wife would be at home. When I said yes, he asked me for my telephone number and began dialling it. All of a sudden I was talking to Di again, this time from the president's desk (the previous time it had been from the desk of the Commissioner of Police). Was I social climbing? I spoke briefly to Di, told her what was required and she said she would get on the next flight to Mahé. René then insisted that the other three should also phone their wives and let them know that we were all fine and being treated well. I was beginning to like this man more and more.

We gave René our verbal acceptance of his offer. We would drop our appeal. But we had to run it past our legal team first. We were driven back to Unionvale in a mood of elation. We would live. The way we had hung on to life and hope through the nightmare of beatings and torture had paid off. Where there is life, there is always hope. I do not think any of us doubted René's word. He was too big a man not to have kept up his side of the bargain. The only niggle was that we might be stuck away somewhere for a very long time while this thing was sorted out. Out of sight, out of mind, as the expression goes. Also because this was a verbal agreement if something did happen to René we had no recourse; this was to become a big worry for not only our legal team but also for some of our families. But this was still better than the prospect of the firing squad or the noose. We felt different men now and this gave us a huge lift; our wives and families now had reason for hope. They had got the good news direct from the president's office. There was a wonderful feeling amongst us as we left for our trip back to our cells, where we could share the good news with the others. The journey back felt so different now. Even the few lights we could see from the vehicle seemed to be shining much brighter. It was almost as if they were putting on a special show for us.

President Albert René addressing the nation

Aubrey Brooks at a press conference

12

The Hijack Trial in Pietermaritzburg

While our trial was in progress in Victoria, another one was taking shape in Pietermaritzburg, the capital of Natal (the province in South Africa where my family and I lived). Colonel Hoare and the rest of the group who had escaped in the Air India Boeing 707 were now on a charge of air piracy, or hijacking.

I knew nothing of this, locked away on Mahé and just getting snatches of local news on our guards' radios; a lot of the broadcast was in Creole anyway. I did not realise either, that the jet that I had heard taking off while I was lying wounded on the hillside, actually had the Colonel and the rest of the group on board. This is what had led up to the trial. I have had to piece together the story from others who were there, including Peter Duffy, and from Colonel Hoare's book, *The Seychelles Affair*. It seems worth retelling briefly because it fills out the picture.

After our little punch up at the gates of Pointe Larue, three lorry-loads of Tanzanian troops had come down the runway from the back gate of the barracks to attack the airport terminal. As they got off the lorries and were advancing on foot, one of our blokes opened fire a bit early, and with that the whole lot of them took to their heels, leaving their weapons and the lorries behind. These were not what you would call crack troops. Then two armoured cars came down the runway, firing on the control tower with their 14.5 mm cannon, causing a lot of damage. One withdrew for some reason, the other got bogged down in mud as it tried to return by road, and our chaps at a roadblock and then took it out with a Molotov cocktail, capturing three of the crew alive. It was dark by now, the airport was secured in a defensive ring and Colonel Hoare intended attacking the barracks again at dawn. Our blokes had lost the element of surprise but the situation was by no means hopeless, as I see it. They had seen how absolutely pathetic the Tanzanians were in action. The captured armoured car crew told them there were only sixty or so soldiers in the barracks anyway. There was no reason why Colonel Hoare and the group should not take the place at first light. There was no way Tanzanian reinforcements could be flown in to an airport that was in our hands. Yet there was nothing to stop Kenyan reinforcements flying in to support us. The control tower operators were by all accounts gibbering wrecks by the time the armoured cars had finished pasting them. One had actually got into a metal dustbin and pulled the lid closed, as if that could protect him against a 14.5 slug that will go through a brick wall. Then somebody at last answered the call from an Air India Boeing that requested permission to land.

This is where the story starts going haywire in several different directions, and which had led to the court case in Pietermaritzburg. Colonel Hoare insists he ordered that the plane be refused permission to land. It would fly into terrible danger because the Seychellois Army and the Tanzanians would presume it to be carrying reinforcements and they would throw everything they had at it. Also, with its civilian passengers, it would be a responsibility and a distraction – presuming it managed to land safely – that Colonel Hoare would rather not have. By the Colonel's own account, the order to refuse the Air India flight landing permission was countermanded by the man ordered to take the instruction to the control tower. The force was made up of individuals, each of them with an impressive military background, but it had never been given the opportunity to mesh and settle into the unquestioning discipline an effective fighting force needs. Individuals were acting as individuals. In a tight spot, some of them saw the arrival of the Air India flight as a possible escape hatch. In the end the aircraft was talked down in good faith by a Rhodesian with experience as a helicopter pilot, who believed he was carrying out the Colonel's orders. It landed, damaging a wing flap against one of the lorries abandoned on the runway. The landing was a hair's breadth from being a catastrophe and this soon came even closer as a 75 mm recoilless rifle began firing at it with increasing accuracy from a hillside a few miles away and mortars started exploding haphazardly on the runway. This civilian aircraft, which had some senior Zimbabweans among its passengers, including the wife of a cabinet minister, came very close to being blown to smithereens on the ground.

Why did the Air India pilot, Captain Saxena, bring down his aircraft in conditions that were so obviously abnormal? Red flares at one end of the runway were ordering him not to land. He was ignored for twenty minutes when he first requested permission to land and then he was talked down by a stranger who clearly did not have much of a clue what he was talking about. I have gone it through again and again with Peter Duffy, Colonel Hoare's second in command, and he is convinced that Saxena was short of fuel. He did not have the option of returning to Harare. Why that should be is a mystery. International regulations require that an aircraft should have enough fuel to return to its airport of origin, or fly on to an alternative. Even twenty minutes of stooging about waiting for an answer from Mahé control tower could surely not explain it. But I am inclined to agree with Duffy. Saxena had more than enough to warn him to turn away. He showed great skill and bravery in bringing the plane in, but he probably had no option. By his own account – and this is confirmed by others – the Colonel was furious at the way his orders had been countermanded. A bad situation could now be made worse by an atrocity against a civilian airliner, with massive casualties. Assisted by the control tower staff, he got in touch by telephone first with the Seychellois Minister of Defence – who was hysterically abusive and dead drunk – and then with a more thoughtful President René himself. René agreed to order a ceasefire and to allow the Air India flight to take off, stipulating the mercenaries should not fly with it.

I believe the Colonel's version of events. He says Saxena offered to fly the group out and, once that happened, the guys just melted away from the Colonel's plan to attack the barracks at first light. Eventually he was left with just a hard core of his Congo comrades – Duffy, Barney and a few others – who were prepared to stick with the plan, and there were not enough for it to be carried out. Eventually, two of his ex-Congo comrades practically marched him on to the plane, which was waiting to take off, having been refuelled under the direction of Duffy, who cheekily signed the fuel requisition 'Lieutenant-General Mickey Mouse'. They flew out with the Tanzanians firing like crazy at them, in spite of René's order, but they did not take a single hit. They headed for Johannesburg but were refused landing permission because of poor weather, and they then altered course for Durban, landing at about 5.00 am.

The rest is history. The incident was treated as a hijacking even though South Africa's minister of law and order, Louis le Grange, initially asked what was wrong with running around in the bush and shooting out a few windows. At the airport in Durban, a senior South African Police officer formally charged the whole group with hijacking. Then they were flown to Pretoria and locked up in Sonderwater Prison under South Africa's security legislation, which did not require them to be brought before a magistrate. Then the police came and took statements, asking them to co-operate so they could get a full understanding of what had gone on. Colonel Hoare and the rest of the group came clean, spilling the beans entirely, believing they were in some kind of debriefing, knowing the government had approved of and supported the coup attempt. They did not dream that their statements would eventually be used against them in a court of law. A very similar situation that we had found ourselves in. They were eventually released from Sonderwater but it soon became clear that the government intended throwing the book at them under the Civil Aviation Act. World pressure was intense, and if they were not charged with air piracy, South African Airways stood to forfeit their landing rights virtually everywhere in the world.

Eventually they stood trial in Pietermaritzburg before the Natal Supreme Court. The case was heard in the old College Road Courthouse – a place where faction-fighting cases were also held (armed conflict between different tribal groups) – probably because the dock was spacious enough to contain large groups of combatants. There is an irony here. I am not a lawyer but piecing things together and reading Colonel Hoare's story, there do seem to have been a few things about that trial that were not fair. Captain Saxena did not give his evidence in Pietermaritzburg, where Colonel Hoare and the others could have prompted their advocate in his cross-examination. It seems the Indian government would not let him go to South Africa, probably because apartheid was still going strong. So he gave evidence in the Seychelles in some kind of weird arrangement where the lawyers went there to get his evidence. Also, his second in command, Captain Misra, was never called as a witness.

I have no doubt that Colonel Hoare was speaking the truth; this was not a hijacking. It was something that happened purely by chance. But the Attorney General of Natal threw the book at Colonel Hoare and the group. The trial dragged on for weeks, just about bankrupting all the defendants, and eventually the court found against the Colonel. The flight had been forced to fly to Durban, the judge and his assessors found. They were guilty of air piracy. The fact that the South African government had been involved was swept under the carpet.

The Colonel got an effective fifteen years in prison. Duffy and two others got five years each, three others got twenty months and the rest got six months. For the Colonel – an officer and a gentleman if ever I saw one – it must have been especially heart breaking and harsh. He sat in jail for years before a combination of remission for good behaviour, age, and a general prisoner amnesty brought him out again. But at least South African Airways kept their landing rights. The irony is that President René pardoned and released us, the people who were actually caught invading his islands, long before Colonel Hoare, Duffy and his comrades were released. (They of course were never pardoned.)

Duffy eventually came out and went back to his old job as a press photographer with the *Sunday Tribune*. One day, Duffy was covering the Ladysmith Agricultural Show, where General Magnus Malan, formerly Chief of the Defence Force and at the time Minister of Defence, was performing the official opening ceremony (Ladysmith had a big army training camp in those days). When the opening ceremony was over General Malan was introduced to the media. When he shook hands with Duffy, he found himself seized in a vice-like grip. Duffy would not let go of his hand.

'When are you going to release my colonel?' asked Duffy.

'Who's your colonel?' Malan said trying to break free.

'Colonel Hoare.' Replied Duffy

'Who are you?' Was the retort from Malan.

'Peter Duffy.' He answered, and with that Malan at last broke free and fled.

As I say, I am not a lawyer and I cannot tell you what the technicalities are of the air piracy case. But one thing I do know: the South African government was in on the invasion plan from the start and Colonel Hoare and the rest of them got a very raw deal.

13

Life in the Communal Prison

Our daily life at Unionvale had always been a lot better than when we were at the mercy of the Tanzanians at Pointe Larue. At Unionvale things were a lot better even though we were still in solitary. Obviously we were not allowed to talk to one another and they policed this very well. However, at least we had bread and tea in the mornings, and fish and rice at lunch and dinner – not very appetising, but exactly what our jailers got. On Sundays we would sometimes get a boiled egg or cubes of pork fat (they did not look too appetising, but the change in taste was always more than welcome) and if we were very lucky the odd apple. You look forward to these small things and when they are denied, it is amazing how it sends your emotions off on a bender – one of our jailers always stole the eggs when he was on duty – becoming a big issue in your life; you get upset. We had two short ablution breaks a day, but no exercise session. We were also no longer handcuffed. It was hard, but not really harsh and the Seychellois people are easy going, not a vindictive bone in their body.

It improved even more when we were put into a communal cell (the old laundry) after the mutiny. Then, once word got about that we had seen the president, it got even more relaxed. Even the food seemed to become a little more varied and appetising. The attitude of the guards changed greatly. Sometimes, when they went off for lunch, they would give us their weapons to look after, for fear the Tanzanians would otherwise steal them (another two plane loads of Tanzanians had flown in since the mutiny). Can you beat it? Prisoners being handed guns for safekeeping in their cell; on one occasion I remember we had two AK 47s ammunition and four-hand grenades left to look after. Go figure! Just a few months earlier if we had made a move to scratch our head we would have been blown away. You would sit there with a gun close at hand and wonder what the next step should be. Take the weapons and make a break for it. We had no locks on the laundry door anyway? But then head to where? This was an island. When the guard came back again, you would hand back his weapon. Everything was very relaxed.

But this was only on the surface (much like a duck, smooth and serine on the surface, whilst its little feet paddle furiously beneath the water in order to propel itself), as you were always on edge. Anything could change in a split second. We had been told our sentences would not be carried out. We would be released when the opportune time came and of course this was all dependent on the president still being in power and alive. So you never knew what was just around the corner. We had a couple of jolts.

Just before Di left the island after the trial, Major Marengo had made a wonderful gesture. He invited her to have lunch with me at Unionvale. The luncheon was set up in the waiting room, with little Bobby Simms acting as waiter complete with a napkin on his arm. It was the usual fish and rice – nothing special – but an emotional encounter and an experience both of us treasure. This was also a lift for the other guys as well. To me it was an example of the tact and thoughtfulness that is so characteristic of the island's people. Not much later an article appeared in *Scope* magazine in Durban. It accurately described Di and I having lunch together; it then went on to say that I was taken to my cell after the lunch and beaten within an inch of my life. This was absolute nonsense. Where *Scope* got it from I still do not know. It must have been planted by somebody with a malicious ulterior motive, but even that I cannot work it out.

Major Marengo was furious. This threatened to undo all the good promised from our meeting with the president; this could derail everything. When he called me in and told me about it, I immediately wrote the president a letter repudiating the *Scope* report, which I gave to the Major. A few days later, Barney, Jerry, Roger and I were told to prepare for an international press conference, which then took place at the palace. The Seychelles government obviously wanted to counter the *Scope* article, and what impressed me most, was that there was no attempt to coach us in advance on what we should or should not say. The press were told to ask whatever questions they wanted. Everything was very open. It went well. We made it clear we were being well treated. We spoke about our role in the mutiny and our releasing of the two officers. However we did it rather low key. We did not want to make ourselves out to be heroes. It seemed to work. Life slipped back into its routine.

But then there came another hiccup. One evening in the middle of October there was some kind of flap in the barracks. The lights were dimmed, and weapons were being issued along with webbing and ammunition. There was the scurrying about that you get in an emergency. People in our situation are always finely attuned to this sort of thing; you pick up all the nuances because anything new can affect your situation. The men jumped into vehicles and sped away. All went quiet again. What was happening?

Then after some hours (that seemed like an eternity), they all came back and it all seemed to pass. In the semi-darkness, looking out of our window, I could see a light on in the office block and I could make out Major Marengo having drinks with some of his colleagues in his office. Only days later did we pick up bits and pieces on the grapevine. The information we gathered was that another South African mercenary had appeared on the island, but had blown himself up with his own bomb. The speculation was that he was here either to spring us from jail or set up another coup attempt. All of which was news to us, as nobody had got any kind of message to us from the outside. As the garbled information came in, the information we received was that a mercenary from Johannesburg named Mike Asher had been killed in his car, along with a local member of the resistance movement. The story that was spread about was that they had accidentally detonated a bomb. What we later heard, was that they had both been shot, after being caught. Their bodies were placed in a car which was then set alight with petrol and then pamphlets from the resistance movement were scattered about the scene. This was done by the security forces in order to make it look like an accident. It looked like a pretty clumsy cover up operation. We never did find out any more about this incident and although it was only supposition on our behalf, I think we were not far from the truth on this one. To this day, I do not know what it was all about and the incident was never raised with us as an issue by the Seychelles authorities. My guess is that Asher was on some sort of reconnaissance mission for the Mancham people; not directly connected with us. Colonel Hoare had his hands full back in Natal, where he was on trial for air piracy. I mention this to illustrate how unpredictable the ups and downs were of the life that we were leading.

We were to have a few a more scares over the next few weeks. One evening a short while after the Asher incident we were laying in our cell when suddenly there was a bloody great explosion from the courtyard area. Bang! The lights went out, guards were running all over the place, much shouting and then as quickly as it started, suddenly silence. A tyre had blown on one of the vehicles in the parking area. On another occasion one Sunday morning there was another huge explosion. Our first reaction was 'shit another coup attempt'; however, this time there had been a controlled blasting taking place on St Anne Island (an island just opposite our prison) and no one had told us to expect it. You sure can get very jumpy in those kinds of circumstances; not only us, but the soldiers were also on edge most of the time. On a lighter side, one day Jerry gave a Tanzanian soldier a neck tie. The soldier immediately put the tie on and he then spent the rest of the day saluting himself in a mirror, much to the amusement of the other guards and ourselves. By now we could sense that we were in the way at Unionvale. Our cells were now full of the mutineers; we were cooped up in the laundry. They did not really know what to do with us. Our former guards were now asking us for food and little favours.

Then at about ten o'clock one morning we were told to get our things together. It had been relatively quiet for a few weeks and although we were now getting on quite well with our new guards, we had no inkling on what was about to happen to us. Once again the mind sets off on another route march.

14
The Flight to Isle de Platte

It had not taken us long to gather our meagre bits and pieces. We were then told to stand by and to await the arrival of Major Marengo, who arrived in a rather jovial mood and I think he could see and feel our apprehension, for he told us to relax. He then said this was the next phase of the conversation we had had with the president a while back. We were going to be flown to an island whilst the trial and all the other issues involving the mutineers were being sorted out. It was a moment that we had been expecting, but things had been so quiet for so long that it had almost slipped our minds. Now that the time had arrived we were not too sure what to think. Was this a good or a bad development? Would we now be put on the island and forgotten? By now it was already the end of October in 1982. Talk about mixed emotions once again. After the Major spoke to us, it was time to say our goodbyes to our former guards, who were now packed into our old cells. It was quite sad and rather surreal. Before long we found ourselves being driven down the now familiar road to the airport. On arrival we were put on the president's personal plane. Nobody told us where we were going, but we all understood this was part of what René had said about getting us out of the way for a time.

The aircraft was a twin-engined Islander. We took off and flew for what appeared to be a very long time; it seemed as if we were never going to get to our destination. All six of us were there: Barney Carey, Jerry Puren, Roger England, Martin Dolinchek, Bobby Simms and me. As I looked down at the vast expanse of the Indian Ocean we were crossing, one thought came to me: escape was almost impossible. We were travelling a very long way indeed. At first I thought that they were deliberately flying us around in order to disorientate us, but on reflection I do not think this ploy was ever necessary.

Then suddenly the tiny coral atoll of Isle de Platte popped into view. My first thought as we circled above, was that we could never land on that. It seemed to be less than two kilometres long and about eight hundred metres wide, an atoll that made a speck of green in the brilliant blue of the ocean. But land we did. The landing strip ran practically the length of the island, through a coconut plantation. It was a grass strip and once the wheels touched down, the gentle drone of the engines was drowned out by the sound of the stones being flicked up as we bounced along the runway. We taxied up to a cluster of buildings beside the runway; here we were told to gather our belongings and wait. From the air it had looked idyllic. On the ground there was not much to see: barracks, officers' mess and dining hall, and a couple of other buildings. I was to discover that the president also had a holiday home on the island. About hundred soldiers manned the outpost and it was considered something of a punishment posting (almost a penal colony). There were no women on the island, no bars or any form of nightlife.

A while later, they walked us through a lush green forest that consisted of a coconut plantation, interspersed with pau-pau (papaya) trees and banana plants. At last fresh fruit; we could not wait. We were then shown our new quarters, a couple of tin huts; these turned out to be appallingly infested with bedbugs and hot as Hades during the day. We were told to settle in and make ourselves comfortable. There were no locks because there was nowhere for us to escape to. We were told to wander down to the army quarters for breakfast, lunch and supper. Apart from that we were on our own. They did however, warn us of the dangers of the stone or scorpion fish and said that should we venture into the ocean, if we were stand on any of these fish, it would be impossible to get us to medical facilities in time and this could mean certain death. 'Welcome to the island'.

The first few days were spent fighting the bedbugs. The camp commander gave us some paraffin and we tried to rub this into our wooden bedsteads to get rid of the bugs. We even got hold of creosote and stood the legs of our beds into tins of this mixture. All this did was let off a very strong smell, and the fumes of the creosote stung our eyes badly. To make matters worse, by now we had already been in confinement for a good while and our skin was no longer used to sunlight, so it did not take too long for all of us to get terribly sun burnt. It was a losing battle. After a number of days, somebody in headquarters had a bright idea and so we were brought back to the army camp; here, there was a small four roomed building standing empty. It had no ablution facilities, and just four rooms that I believe had previously been the old senior NCOs' quarters. We were shown to the building and having just left the heat of our tin hut, this place was like a palace. After storing our belongings, we were told that we would have to go to the north of the island after breakfast every day; we were to return for lunch at midday and come back in the evening for supper and to sleep. This would keep us out of the way of the troops and whatever they did during the day. This was now going to be our new home and we began to settle in. How long would it be for, weeks, months or even years? There was no telling. However, we finally had a place that we could call our own, a small step but a great feeling. When we closed ourselves in our cell that first night, we could not even begin to wonder what the future would hold for us, way out here in the middle of the Indian Ocean, out of sight and mind of the rest of the world. Would we be forgotten?

Life improved greatly. The Seychelles really is paradise on earth. There are theories that the Seychelles were the original Garden of Eden, and that could be right. I certainly would never argue against that. We got the same food every day – fish and rice, tea, pieces of pork on a Sunday, eggs at times – and it was exactly the same as the soldiers ate. But now we also had paw-paws and bananas that were growing on the island, loads of fresh fish and there were plenty of coconuts. We found a number of ways of eating and cooking coconut: we ate them raw, roasted them, made sweets, syrup, a kind of toffee, and found that when you let a coconut ferment for a while, the inner part starts to produce its own nutrients (in order to feed the young plant once the nut had fallen to ground); it was like eating ice cream, absolutely delicious and very nutritious. A month or two after arriving on the island, we discovered a few chilli bushes and this also added to our ability to change the taste of our food. We were in very good condition physically. The diet of fish had been really good for us, and by now we had all lost a fair amount of weight and we were feeling much better for it. I found an old vehicle's front axle lying in the undergrowth; I cleaned it up and made it into a barbell. I set up my own open-air gymnasium, and I did curls, squats, press ups, lifts and other exercises every day without fail. Along with running on the beach daily, I was in good shape.

Nearly every day Barney and I would wade out to the coral reefs. This was absolutely fascinating. At low tide you can walk out for miles into the azure blue Indian Ocean. The water is crystal clear. The sand almost pure white and dotted about were all the different coloured coral and a wide variety of sea life, from beautiful fish (both to eat and look at), to moray eels, shells, star fish, and sea cucumbers etc… We often saw sharks and giant rays – you took your chances. Out on the reefs there were also giant clams (the largest shell fish in the world); they can grow up to a metre wide (at the hinges). One morning Barney shoved a stick into one of these open clams and although it shut its jaws slowly, once they were closed there was nothing we could do to pull out the stick, and it was there for days. Imagine getting your leg trapped in one of those and the tide coming in. We fished with hand lines, made spears and learnt to spear fish; we caught a lot of different species and we only caught fish to eat. There is a species of shell fish that the Seychellois call Sikori. These have rather large shells between six and ten inches long and once you catch them, you place a hook through the mollusc and hang them, with the shell facing downwards. It is a rather funny sight, seeing these shells hanging from trees like fruit. After a few days the shell will fall off and leave the meat exposed. It is now ready to cook and they do taste really good. But mainly we collected seashells.

The Seychelles have the most beautiful shells – giant cowries, grading down to the miniatures, and all kinds of other species – and we started our own collection. For this we had to get President René's permission through the army commander, because law on the islands protects shellfish. But permission came and I think the soldiers were impressed and a bit envious because they were not allowed to take shellfish. With this came a new problem: during the day while we were up on the north of the island the guards started stealing our shells. One could hardly blame them as just a few of our shells would be of the same value as their monthly salary; we then asked the commander for a padlock, so our belongings would be safe and he obliged. We locked ourselves in every night. I think we must have been the only prisoners in the world who locked themselves in at night and locked our jailers out during the day. Barney and I made a proper collection which we recorded quite thoroughly. We were not experts and we gave the shells our own names, until one day, during a visit from the British High Commissioner, Barney and I were given a book that Di had sent us. The book contained all the scientific names. We then corrected our catalogue. It took some time but there again as a prisoner time is something you have plenty of. In fact, any diversion to fill the day is always welcome.

The High Commissioner came to visit us from time to time and he would bring us food parcels, letters and that kind of thing (I think he visited us twice or it may even have been three times during our stay on Isle de Platte). On one of his visits in the middle of May he arrived with some snorkelling equipment and underwater goggles and so forth. For Barney and me this was the best thing that could have happened. Now we could explore the reefs properly every day and it was a magical new world that opened up for us. You could swim out over the reef in crystal clear water, and then watch the seabed just fall away below as you swam away from the shore. It felt as if you were flying over an escarpment in a light aircraft. It was a fantastic sensation. You could swim out into really deep water, where the sea was a deep purple, and you could then dive down quite deep and swim towards the shore. As you got closer to the beach, the seabed got lighter and lighter, and the clear water then exposed all the coral and wonderful sea life below. Occasionally you would think about the sharks and other things that must be cruising about. Thinking about this you would head back towards the reef pretty fast with the hairs on the back of your neck standing on end.

We also did our bit for conservation. There were lots of turtles that nested on the island, both the Hawksbill and the Green turtles. The Green turtles were known in Creole as the 'Torti d'Mer' and it was these that the soldiers liked to hunt, as they make very tasty eating. I liked the meat myself, but I did not like the way the turtles were hunted. During the night the females (they could weigh up to 200 kgs) would come ashore to lay their eggs and on their journey from the water's edge, to their nesting place, they would leave flipper marks on the sand. In the morning the soldiers would follow the marks to her nest in the dunes, and then kill her as she was laying her eggs (there could be between 100 and 150 eggs in the nest). It was very cruel and it obviously meant thousands of new turtles would not hatch. So Barney and I would go on a beach patrol in the early mornings and sweep away any flipper marks in order to make it difficult for the soldiers to find the nests. On one occasion we found one of these nests where the female had been taken from and decided to cook the eggs in order to add something new to our diet. After boiling the eggs for nearly two and a half hours we finally abandoned this exercise, as they looked and felt like jelly filled ping pong balls.

It was no great hassle when one day a new commander arrived and decided prisoners should not spend the day lolling around, but that they should be made to do some useful work. He told us that he wanted us to keep a vegetable garden to supplement the garrison diet. He would supply the seeds and equipment; all we had to do was grow the vegetables. We knew that the soldiers already kept a vegetable patch, but this we would make special. Anything, to help fill the day would be most welcome. We went into this new task with great enthusiasm and soon we had a flourishing vegetable garden about a quarter of an acre in size. We had everything – carrots, cucumbers, lettuces, onions and beetroot, that kind of thing. The Seychelles is so fertile that anything grows. It improved the diet, not only for us, but for the soldiers as well. Quite a while later a new problem arose: we began to get caterpillars and other bugs that were destroying the vegetables. We asked the guard commander if he could get us some insecticide. He came back with a tin of defoliant. Gerry explained that this was the wrong thing and that it would actually destroy the garden worse than any caterpillars. However, he thought we were trying to undermine his authority and would hear nothing of it.

'What do you know? You are only a mercenary. I am the guard Commander. I know best. Just do as you are told and use it on the garden,' he ordered, making a big show of it. He then turned on his heels and strutted away.

We were at a loss. This was crazy. But some of the soldiers who had watched the encounter could see we had no intention of following orders. To avoid an incident they mixed the defoliant with water themselves and put it on the garden that night. The next day the entire garden was like a mini-desert, exactly as we had said it would happen. Not only had all the island's inhabitants been deprived of some excellent vegetables, but we had also lost our garden and with that another time consuming project that we had all found very rewarding. There was now an embarrassing silence all round and nobody ever mentioned the vegetable garden again.

We got to know our guards, though they no longer were really guarding us, as it was more as if we just shared the island with them. There were some wonderful characters. One was Ralph, who oddly enough, had been in the group when I was first arrested and interrogated after my capture. Ralph was forever on the island, for no sooner was his stint on the island over and he was returned to the mainland, that he would be returned to the island, because he was always in trouble with the army. He could not take anything seriously. When they had a flag-raising ceremony he would waltz out on the parade ground, waggling his bum and then he would stand at attention and salute with both hands. Ralph was not made for military life. He became a great friend. On a few occasions he gave us some 'mampoer' (a type of liquor made from coconuts), which was illegally distilled on the island. Whilst it did not taste so great it certainly had a bit of a kick and you would feel a bit merry after having one or two. This had to be done without the commander finding out. One day Ralph called me to one side and gave me a wooden carving of a miniature pirogue (a type of fishing boat) that he had carved for me and a few weeks later he presented me with a small fish creel he had also made. I still have them to this day.

Another character was a tiny, coal-black private who we knew as Mad Mike Hoare. He was on the island as punishment because he had got very drunk in a bar on Mahé one night, brandished his army rifle and declared he was Mike Hoare and that he was there to take over the island. For that he was packed off to Isle de

Platte – the Seychelles Army seemed to have a sense of irony – and he would become very indignant whenever he related this amusing incident to us. We found him to be quite a hoot.

Life was improving all the time. During the second of his visits the British High Commissioner brought us a transistor radio, which amazingly they allowed us to keep. He also gave me two photographs (with no captions or an accompanying letter). One was of our youngest son standing in front of a Christmas tree next to a bicycle, with two broken arms, and the other was a picture of my wife, with a young lady holding a baby. For many months both of these photographs were to worry me quite a bit. This was because I could never fathom out what had happened to our son or who the young lady with the baby was. On this visit we were also given a goody parcel for Christmas. This contained lots of items like toiletries, vitamins, biscuits, sweets, etc. and with these, and a couple of ice cold beers that the guards had given us, we settled down to our first Christmas meal in two years. We wore our paper hats, said grace, made toasts to our families and friends, and then tucked in to a most unusual meal, under the most unusual circumstances. The menu read:

> Pork Creole
> Rice Piquant
> Christmas Pudding (Nestles)
> Cocoanut Flambé
> Vitamin C Effervescent (Orange)
> Isle de Platte – Christmas 25 December 1982

It was definitely a grand occasion. On one or two other occasions the six of us got merry in the evening with a bottle of brandy from the guards or some of the local skokiaan or mampoer, which was a wonderful treat. But you can imagine what a small amount of alcohol it took for us to get on our ear, not to mention the massive headache the next day.

Over that period there were a lot of news broadcasts, many in Creole or French, and occasionally we would hear the word 'mercenaries', but it all seemed to be about the trial of Colonel Hoare and the others in Pietermaritzburg. Had we had been forgotten? At the beginning of our stay on the island we were allowed to go to the president's holiday home and watch videos of the football world cup on the president's own television set. Could this happen anywhere but the Seychelles? Sadly this would not last long, as when the new guard commander arrived he soon put a stop to it. One Saturday in early November we heard an aircraft approaching; this was unusual as the normal bi-weekly flights were usually on Thursdays. We never gave it much thought as we made our way slowly back from the vicinity of the president's house to the camp for breakfast, when suddenly, from around the corner, President René himself appeared along with Major Marengo and a handful of civilians. He was dressed in a pair of shorts, casual shirt, sandals and was wearing a large sombrero. He gave us a short cheerful wave and moved on. We went back to our quarters after breakfast and wondered what had brought him to the island. The mind went walkabout again. I thought he was looking very pale and tense. He sat speaking to the army officers for a while and then he came across and spoke to us.

He said, 'Gentlemen are you enjoying your holiday? You are all looking tanned and fit. They are obviously taking good care of you.' But that was it, a very brief encounter. He did not say anything about his plans for our future. We waited to hear some news, any news, nothing happened and a short while later we heard the aircraft take off. We never did find out the reason for his brief visit.

It was a relaxed life. We got on well with our guards. I think there was some sort of unwritten law and as long as we did not overstep the mark, all would be fine; however, put it to the test and it would be at your peril. The greatest challenge was how to cope with boredom. Gathering fruit or looking for new berries in the plantation was always a very pleasant task and as you walked among the palm trees, a wide variety of birds would fly alongside you only inches away from your grasp, as they had no fear of humans. It was an incredible thing to experience. But as condemned prisoners there was always an undercurrent of fear. On one occasion we returned to our quarters to find our guards standing in little huddles. There was a lot of shouting and gesticulating going on and the first thing you thought was 'what now'. Once it had all quietened down we were to find that it was nothing too sinister. One of the guards had found and killed an albatross and this had thrown the camp into total disarray, for there was a very strong belief that killing one of these birds would bring terrible bad luck to everyone on the island, and this was the last thing we needed. We did however get to see one of these magnificent birds. They have the largest wing span of all sea birds (the span on a Wandering Albatross can be up to two metres) and using the thermals they can remain up in the air (often at great altitudes) for a whole day without flapping their wings, but sadly they only lay one egg a year.

Every now and then a new group of soldiers would arrive and sometimes they would be overtly hostile toward us. Weekends we did not enjoy very much, as the newcomers, who were already very unhappy at being on the island anyway, would sometimes get drunk and become very aggressive; then from the stillness of the night, the shouting would erupt and from the darkness outside you could hear them shouting, such as, 'Hey mercenaire, we have come to carry out the death penalty', and yet another would shout, 'We will save our government money and kill you now'.

Invariably, the soldiers that were already on the island would try to defuse the situation; this would sometimes create further eruptions with more shouting and banging of tables etc. Although this was not often, we were very glad of the padlock on our door. One day there was a big flap as a warship sailed close to the shore. The troops were convinced it was a South African ship come to rescue us (some chance!) and with much shouting and glaring at us, they finally yelled at us to get back in our cells and they were off down to the beach with rifles and machineguns ready to open up – small arms fire versus naval guns (that would have been interesting). It turned out in the end that it was a Soviet ship. But things could have turned very nasty for us if there had been one trigger happy soldier there. During another period they decided that an attempt to spring us from the island was imminent and so they placed big logs all along the runway. This was a labour intensive exercise and the obstacles had to be cleared every Thursday. Once we pointed out that if they did come to get us off the island it would probably be with the use of a helicopter, they saw the wisdom in this and the pointless exercise was put to an end.

It was during this period that there was a lot of talk about how the world could end during the upcoming equinox tides. We had heard on the radio that the planets were going to be aligned for the first time in so many thousands of years and this could cause earth to be pulled off its axis. There was a lot of talk amongst the guards. A couple of days before the full high tides were due, the guards spotted a most unusual sight out at sea. It was the start of a water spout and as it built in size it appeared to be making its way towards us. At first it was not too intimidating, but as it got closer and closer to us, we all began to wonder if in fact there was not an element of truth in this disaster that had been forecast. We became mesmerised by this gigantic funnel that was coming out of the sea and swirling up into the heavens and that was now snaking its way towards us. It was breath taking. I am sure that it was many miles away, but it felt very, very close indeed. What a sight to behold. It eventually made its way to the east of our island and finally disappeared. A few days later the equinox spring tides did arrive and by now we were all a bit jumpy. The name of the island, Isle de Platte is self-explanatory, flat island (at its highest point it could not have been more than a few metres high), so at high tide there was not much left of the island. We were all very glad when this little period was over. Life was a roller coaster any way you looked at it.

On another day a coconut fell out of a tree and hit Barney. At first it looked quite comical; there was a hollow thud as it hit him square in the middle of his head and then his eyelids flickered as he slowly started to do a pirouette before tumbling to the ground. It did however turn out to be quite serious, as he was unconscious for a good few minutes. The army commander was as worried as we were; it seems he had been told to take special care of us, as we had now become pretty valuable goods. This incident brought home to us how far away from everything we were. No hospitals, no medical care if anything went seriously wrong. Barney and I went out on the reefs every day. Tread on a stonefish, which has venom worse than a mamba, and that would be it: curtains, and an agonising death before you could get back to shore. Then there was the endless planning, storing of foodstuff, looking for containers to hold water, etc. just in case an opportunity for an escape of some kind ever presented itself. This was never far from our mind; it also gave something to focus on. But it never happened. We were fit and well fed. We were convinced that somewhere the cogs were turning and someday, if the president kept his word, we would be flown out of there to rejoin our families, whom by now, we knew only from the odd photographs that were brought out to us every now and then by the British High Commissioner.

Every second Thursday, we were teased even more. The supply aircraft would fly in every two weeks on a Thursday, regular as clockwork, carrying provisions and new personnel. It would taxi to the end of the runway at our end of the island where it would be parked ready for take-off. The pilot always left the keys in the ignition. We had observed this closely. Barney, Roger, Jerry and I were all qualified pilots. We could fly that aircraft and it was always parked tantalisingly close to where we would spend our day. All we had to do was get in and go, while the pilot and the others were preoccupied. We would have to take the plane past the military barracks, about halfway down the airstrip, but we would have surprise on our side, and they would still have to get the firearms out of the makeshift armoury, where they were kept during the day. I am sure that they did not believe that we were licensed pilots. But then what? We did not even know where we were. We did not know if any friendly airfield was within range. Where could we make for, the American base at Diego Garcia? (We were later to find out that it was due east of where we were.) Was it in range? Could we find a compass bearing? We argued the thing back and forth, week after week. What would happen if we had to put the aircraft down in the sea? All these were unknowns. In the end we did nothing, because actually we had no idea what we would do once we found ourselves in the air. Could you trade the likelihood of being pardoned and released against a crazy risk like this? Back and forth the discussion went. From the forest we would eye those keys hanging in the ignition. Vaguely we formulated an idea that if our condition deteriorated sharply we would seize the moment. Until then we would wait. It was like having a card in reserve – a weakish card, but still a card. We bided out time. One day ran into the next. We survived. We could be there for years, perhaps even decades. Had the world had forgotten us?

In the prison garden on Isle de Platte from left:
Aubrey Brooks, Martin Dolinchek, Roger England, Jerry Puren, Bernard Carey and Bob Sims

THE FLIGHT TO ISLE DE PLATTE 97

The six of us on the veranda of our prison home on Isle de Platte

The six of us at a press conference on Isle de Platte prior to our release

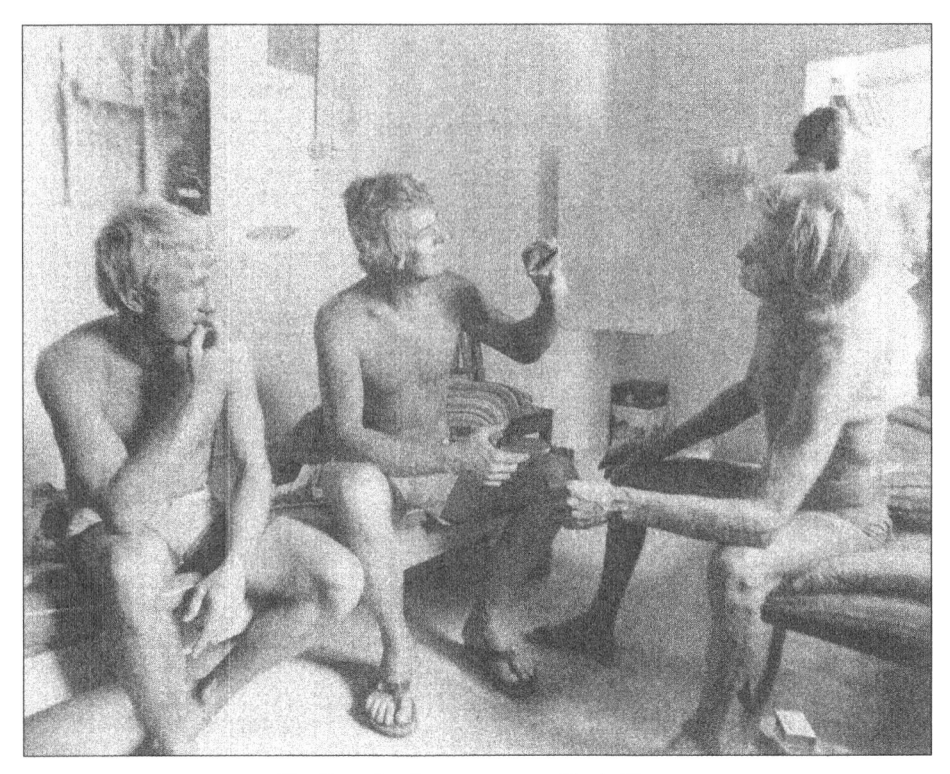

The four of us in our room on Isle de Platte

15

News of our Return to Mahé and the Pardon

We had been about nine months on Isle de Platte. By now we had got used to our daily routine, which was pleasant enough in its way, but there seemed to be no end to it. Then one morning out of the blue, the camp commander, Major Montague, came over to us as we were having breakfast. This was fairly unusual and we wondering what had gone wrong, when in a cheerful voice, he said, 'Gentleman, get yourselves cleaned up and looking at your best, you are going to attend an international press conference here on the island this morning.' This was astounding news and our spirits were raised immediately.

Something must be in the offing. We had mixed emotions: excitement, anticipation, and even fear; as went about readying ourselves, we were on tenterhooks. It was 12 July 1982 – I will never forget that date – and we waited for what seemed an eternity. Every now and then we thought we could hear an aircraft approaching and then nothing. Finally, out of the clear blue sky, we watched in anticipation as the aircraft finally landed and slowly taxied, making its way towards us in the camp precinct. On board was a team of journalists from the British newspaper, *Mail on Sunday*, amongst them a reporter named Sarah Gibson and a photographer named Keith. Seychelles television was there as well. We had been told to get into our best gear and we met them under two large fig trees in front of the officers' quarters. It was a very light hearted conference; they asked about our life on the island, how we were being treated, that kind of thing. They took pictures of us in all kinds of settings, including the soldiers' vegetable garden (ours had been killed by the defoliant). We co-operated, of course, but we could not really understand the point of it all. We had not been given any reason for the interview or what was happening. We assumed that it was another attempt at getting some more good publicity for the Seychelles.

With the press meeting finished, they then started a photo shoot. It was then that Sara, a good-looking, attractive, fair-haired, vivacious girl with a very nice manner, managed to get me alone for a moment and asked, 'When do you think you'll be leaving?'

'I just don't know,' I replied.

'What if I told you this week?' was her response.

'Lady, I would think that you've flipped your lid,' I said.

'Keep this quiet. I'll talk to you later,' she quietly whispered, as other people approached.

My mind was in a spin. Who was this girl? What did she know? Was she playing games with me? Later, while we were showing her and the others our shell collection she asked if we could show her the area where we were collecting the shells from. The Major agreed. This turned out to be a ploy to get to speak to us alone. Once we had arrived at our beach site, she pulled Barney and me aside again and said, 'We're helping to put this whole lot together, to make it possible for you to get out of here, possibly even next week.'

I was stunned. I still did not know whether to believe her. Then a Seychelles Officer, who had come with the press group, approached me. He pulled me to one side. I was expecting the worse; maybe he had overheard us. But then very awkwardly, he started asking me questions. He could not come straight out with what was on his mind, but he asked things like, if the others and I needed an airfare home, how would we be able to pay for it? He looked embarrassed and uncomfortable. So Sarah was on the level. 'Our families would pay no question about it,' I said. He nodded, made some small talk and then rejoined the rest of the party. By now my heart was pounding and I could not wait to tell the others. This just seemed to cement what Sarah had just said.

When the party had left, we told the others and everyone was gob smacked. After all these months, could it be real? Was somebody playing tricks on us? There was much excitement and making of plans, wondering how and when it would be done. The mind went on a route march all of its own; sleep was almost impossible. Now began the waiting period again, as we had not been given any further details. One day passed, then a second and on the third day, the president's plane arrived. We were told to get our belongings together quickly and get on board. I think it took us about five minutes to gather our belongings. As prisoners, we travelled light. All I had to round up was my shell collection, some trinkets I had made, a couple of carvings and there we were. It was ironic, for as we were preparing to leave, the first batch of our former jailers were now arriving on the island. They had arrived on the same aircraft that we were about to fly out in. They had come to start their sentences for the part in they played in the mutiny. Their trial had by now been completed and they were to serve their time on the very island where we had been kept. The guards wanted to give us a good farewell and so they went and collected a little petrol driven tipper, into which they loaded our meagre belongings and offered us a lift in the dumpster. On our way to the aircraft, we said our goodbyes to our former jailers and bade them well. It just goes to show that life has many twists and turns, so no matter how bad things are, you never know what awaits you just around the corner. My mind flashed back to the time just before my capture, when I had contemplated taking my own life. As I say, it was just a flash back, for as quickly as I had the thought, in an instant it was gone. My how the wheel does turn.

It was like a dream. There we were belting down the runway in the plane we had often thought of stealing. Once we had lifted off, the pilot flew us around the island so that we could say goodbye and there below us was Isle de Platte, our home of nine months, disappearing from view. The strange thing is that I felt a kind of sadness. I think all of us did. We were leaving behind friends: Ralph, 'Colonel Hoare' and the others. They had become part of our lives. Barney and I were leaving the coral reefs we had come to know so well. We were overjoyed because it now seemed clear we were going to be pardoned and sent home to our families, but I think that even today, a part of every one of us stayed behind on Isle de Platte.

When we landed on Mahé, we were not taken back to Unionvale, but to the Police Headquarters in Victoria where Commissioner James Pillay met us. This was highly significant. The police in the Seychelles are an elite force, very well trained and aware of people's rights the way an army never can be. Our anticipation was correct. We were to be pardoned. The president wanted to see us in person. We were put into unlocked cells at the police station, and for us this was the nearest thing to being in a hotel. It was unbelievable almost like a dream. We did not see too many people when we first arrived, but those that did catch a glimpse of us, waved and gave us a cheery smile. Later that afternoon we were taken up to the commissioner's office and he gave us a formal welcome and told us we would be having a meeting with the president the next day. Although he never told us what was going on, he gave us a knowing smile as he handed us each a drink while he put on some music. It was a James Last record, another moment I will never forget. We had a very jovial and happy hour with James Pillay. He remarked how well we were all looking and I felt that he was genuinely happy for us. That first night they asked if we would like to order our food from the takeaway, chicken and chips, burger… unbelievable!

The new day dawned and Barney, Jerry, Roger and I – the four under sentence of death – were taken to see René to receive our pardons. To call it an emotional occasion is not quite adequate. We had been on what amounted to death row for sixteen months. But now everything had changed. We were going back to our wives and families. This terrible nightmare was nearly over. René spoke to us. I did not quite take in all he was saying as I was so choked up, but he was wishing us well. Then, as we were all about to leave, he asked if Barney and I could stay. To me, he said, 'There are no conditions to your release, as you know. But I would like to have your word that you will never again cause harm to these islands or their people.'

'Mr President,' I said. 'You have my word.'

I meant it. I have the highest regard for René. In my mind he was and still is, a very compassionate man, with a very big heart. I am sure that he must have taken a lot of flak on our behalf over the preceding months. I am still not sold on socialism but I can see now it is not quite what I was brainwashed to believe. If people want socialism, let them have socialism. René might have got in by a coup, but he did later hold an election and win it. Fair is fair, and, what about the Seychellois people? I had found them to be the friendliest, most fun-loving people.

Then he said he would like to speak to Barney alone. I thanked him again and left to wait with the others. Unfortunately for Barney, it went very differently. René sadly told him the news that he had not heard whilst he was a prisoner. His wife had divorced him during the months that we were in prison. René said he could not leave him to discover the news only when he got home. He is a very kind man, a very human person.

Barney was absolutely devastated. He was never quite the same again and the news shook all of us. But it could not dim the fact that we were going to live; we were about to be freed and we would soon be back with our families. When Commissioner Pillay told us we would be flying out on British Airways (nobody suggested Air Swaziland), our hearts skipped a beat because that flight was next day. But no – we were booked for a week later. A week! How could we wait a week? But in the end the time went by very quickly. We had a number of visitors over the next few days. All kinds of people came to visit us at the police station: Betsy the nurse who had saved Barney and me in hospital; people who had guarded us at various stages; and the policewoman who had tried to give me water on the night I was captured. We had become celebrities. One person, who did not come to visit, was the evil Tanzanian bastard who had beaten us and tried to shoot us in hospital. I had told him that the moment they took my off handcuffs, I would strangle him with my bare hands and the odd thing is, that from the day they removed my handcuffs I never saw him again.

Then at last the day arrived. In the early hours of the morning and after saying our farewells to all at the police headquarters, we were each put into a car along with the officer who had been responsible for our interrogation and were then driven from the police station through town to the airport. It was the most amazing thing. People turned out in their hundreds to cheer us; it was like a ticker-tape parade. I often wonder about that. If they were so fond of us mercenaries, why did they later vote René into power? We had come to topple him. It did not quite add up. Maybe we had added a little excitement to their lives. But I think mainly it was relief that things had turned out this way: that we were not to be executed. The Seychellois are very kind, gentle people. They would shrink from anything like that; it would have been on their conscience.

The aircraft had been waiting for a long time for us; all the other passengers were in transit so they were already on board. Another international press conference had been hurriedly put together at the airport. The press conference was a very light-hearted affair and a few jokes were made about us travelling in economy class and Martin Dolinchek flying in business class. I think this action also cemented in the minds of the Seychellois, that the South African government was involved and that they were looking after their own. We finally walked out onto the apron and at the bottom of the stairs we shook hands with the officers, both the military and the police as they too bade us farewell. As I got to the top of the stairs I turned and looked back at this group of people standing on the tarmac and at the people in the building waving to us and another look at the island that had become home for so long. There was no resentment, only touch of sadness in my heart. As I stepped into the aircraft I closed a chapter behind me. I then looked forward and wondered what the future may hold. The wonderful airhostesses, with their cheerful smiles, took us to our seats. The quietness of the aircraft was suddenly broken with loud cheers and much hand clapping. This followed an announcement by the Captain of the British Airways flight, in which he had apologised to everyone for the delay in departure and had welcomed us to freedom. It was one of the most amazing feelings. After take-off, he flew a figure-of-eight over Mahé to give us a good look at the place where we had been held for so long. From the air Barney and I could see how close we had been to each other on the hillside, during that fateful firefight, those years ago.

It was champagne treatment all the way on the flight to Johannesburg. Then a media siege at the airport. Di flung herself into my arms and our sons were there; as were many family friends and a very large crowd that had turned up to welcome us back. My head was buzzing with it all. The *Sunday Times* newspaper was still looking after us and they put us up in a hotel in Johannesburg for a couple of days, and then eventually we flew back to Durban to start putting our lives together again. I was still in a daze. Somehow I had survived. I was back with my family. I could not have survived without my faith in God, my wonderful family, friends, the many people who had prayed for us and the excellent training I had received from my military unit the Selous Scouts.

The six of us at police headquarters

104 DEATH ROW IN PARADISE

The four mercenaries (sentenced to death) at a press conference

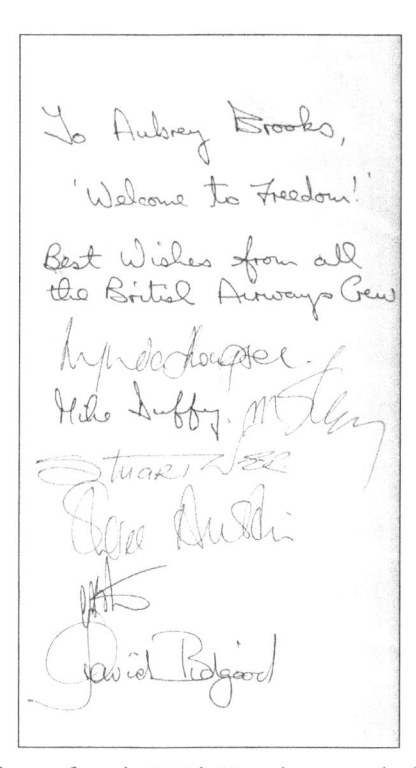

The signed menu from the British Airway's crew on the flight home

16
Diane's story
(by Diane Brooks)

'I'm going to do a "funny".' This was the first I heard of the operation. My only reply was, 'Where? As long as it is not against Zimbabwe, as that is the only country, you could be had up for high treason. No don't tell me, the less I know the better.' Little did I know these words would come back to haunt me.

There were several meetings all over the show, which I did not go to. On one occasion, however, we went to the infamous Riviera Hotel, where I met Barney, who was, on first impression a very smooth dude. I was told he was high up in the operation and that he had worked in the Congo. There were a few other guys there, but I did not take too much notice of them, save to get to know Ken and Karen Dalgleish. My next clear memory was at Louis Botha airport. I was rather worried that Aubrey (Aubs) would not get back from this venture in time, as my parents were flying out for a holiday within the next three weeks.

Barney jokingly said, 'Of course, we will be back or we could end up sun burnt with stripes from the bars of the jail cell on our faces.' At that point Barney gave me a coin, just before they boarded the plane.

Looking at the coin after the plane had taken off, I noticed that it was from the Seychelles. I was not even sure where this place was; I had only vaguely heard of it from travel magazines. Later that night I looked it up in the atlas. Little did I know…

Time passed by and my story to the rest of the world was that Aubs had gone overseas on business. The night that everything went wrong, we (Rory, Roy and I) went to dinner with the parents, Paunchy and Mom Chapman, of good friends of ours. All through dinner I was incredibly nervous. I thought it was because of the big storm that was brewing outside, with thunder and lightning flashing across the sky. I just could not wait to get home and during the car ride back I said to our son Rory, 'Something is wrong, I can just feel it.' At home I was like a cat on a hot tin roof and could not relax; I even cleaned the stove at midnight just to try to switch off.

Roy was also restless that night and insisted on sleeping in our bed. Dawn finally broke and everyone was at sixes and sevens, nothing went right, everything was running so late; I did not even have time to listen to the radio. I dropped the boys off at school. Then I went to the Umbogintwini Post Office to clear the mailbox.

Included in the mail was a certified slip; it was for the earrings Aubs had ordered for me. I decided what the hell I'm late anyway, so I should go inside and collect them. While waiting in the queue the people around me were highly agitated. There had been a problem at the airport. While I was being served, a driver from a nearby factory came in and said that an aircraft had been hijacked last night and that due to this they had all been called out during the night; he also said there were at least three dead people on board. On hearing this, I asked him, 'Where had the aircraft been hijacked from?'

He told me there had been an attempted coup in the Seychelles and that the mercenaries had hijacked an Air India plane. My head started spinning. All I could think about was getting out of there quickly, before anyone noticed my reaction. I drove to work somehow and immediately phoned Alex and Eve Gibson (a couple who we had known for many years, later become my Durban Mom and Dad) and all I said was, 'Come quick something has happened.' They were there within minutes.

I told them what I knew and that I wanted to go to the viewing area overlooking the airport in order to see the aircraft, which by now had been parked at the end of the runway closest to the view point. When I saw the aircraft, I just knew Aubs was not on it. The days passed in a haze, with conflicting stories coming from the firemen who worked at the airport; they told Tony, Aubrey's business partner (who they knew quite well, as only a couple of weeks before they had both been working at the airport selling life insurance), that they had seen Aubs getting off the plane. Alex and Eve moved into the house so we (the boys and I) would not be alone. On the Saturday night, the reporters started phoning. I still had no idea what had happened to Aubs. Was he in Durban? What if he was still acting like a tourist, and if his name was printed in the newspaper would they then arrest him? I wanted the whole thing to be kept quiet and kept denying everything, saying Aubs would have a good laugh when he returned from his business trip to Europe. One reporter (Ron Goulden) in particular was really persistent and came knocking on the door wanting to get a photo for the front page of the Sunday newspaper. He even managed to get into the flat attached to the house and tried to force the door open, by which point I had hidden under a bed. Thank goodness I had sent the boys to sleep at a friend's house. The siege ended when our cat, Gypsy, jumped off the balcony onto Ron's back and clawed him to pieces; with that he took off and I never saw him again.

Alex wanted to get out of the house in order to get a copy of the newspaper and at the same time he did not want to have his photo in the press as he also needed to return to Zimbabwe and any involvement with the Seychelles incident would have created problems for him on his return. So later that night, he slipped out wearing my wig. We did laugh when we saw him kitted out with the wig and sunglasses. By now the news was full of the mercenaries who had returned on the Air India aircraft. Firstly about them being arrested and then after a week their pending release. The release was due to be done the day before my Mom and Dad would be arriving; so Aubs would make it back before they came, like he promised. The next day I was upstairs making the beds in readiness for their arrival, when I heard my name being called from downstairs; I ran downstairs, thinking it was Aubs and half way down I saw one of the group standing there. My mind raced. Why was he there? Had something happened? Had Aubs been the one killed? Had he been left behind? I heard someone shouting.

'NO, NO', and then I realised it was me.

I numbly heard that Aubs had been shot and captured. I then refused to hear anymore. Eve bundled me off to the doctor. I was in shock. I was given a strong sedative, which should have knocked me out, but no, the mind would not switch off and I sat through the long night wondering what to do. When the morning broke, I knew that today my Mom and Dad would arrive and so far, they knew nothing of what had happened. How would my Mom react? You see my Mom had been a prisoner in a Japanese prisoner of war camp during World War II, and she was very sensitive about reliving that period of her life. I then learnt what a good actor I really could be. Between Alex and Eve, and Tony (a neighbour and work colleague of Aubs), we devised a plan: they would take me to the airport under the pretence that my car had broken down. The second car was there to collect the luggage. My folk's arrival was very a very happy moment. Then my Mother asked where Aubs was. I did not want to lie. This was neither the time nor the place, so I made as if I had not heard her. Fortunately for me there was a timely diversion: they had discovered that my Dad's suitcase had gone missing and this presented a new problem. Quite a while later we arrived home and with suitable liquid refreshment, I asked my Mom where her pills were. My father gave me a strange look when I asked my Mom to go and get them. I then said to my Dad that there is no easy way to say this, but I think the newspaper would say it best and with that I handed him the local morning paper with the story of Aubrey making headlines. Once Mom and Dad had settled down, they were terrific and they were full of praise for my cool handling of the situation on their arrival.

That night the television news showed the footage of the captured mercenaries.

It was a real low moment, seeing Aubs so badly beaten and with his leg shot up. What followed was really amazing: flowers and cards began arriving from all over the country and from people I did not even know. This went on for a number of weeks; they were truly a great comfort to me. The next weeks and months I did not handle so coolly. I did not know the correct course of action to take, and due to the training from the Rhodesian Bush War days I decided to keep a very low profile and wait. I just wanted to protect the two boys from the press and prying gossips. So they spent a lot of time with friends. I refused to leave the house, convinced that I would receive a phone call from Aubs. After many weeks the phone did ring, and guess what, it was Aubs. It was so strange and it was like a normal everyday phone call. He assured me that he was well and that I could write to him c/o the police. I then informed my very tolerant parents that everything would now be OK and that we could now go out and do the shopping. I bought a new pair of red shoes that day, and sat down to write a very carefully worded letter.

Then one morning the phone rang and it was Mike Hoare and he invited me out to lunch. Prior to this I had never met him. On his arrival, I was instantly struck by his commanding presence. This was a man who commanded respect and was an absolute gentleman. We drove to Durban and had lunch at a French restaurant; Peter Duffy also arrived and joined us for lunch. One of the courses that we had for lunch was duck; this, Peter pointed out, was not 'Wild Geese' (a reference to the former mercenary unit that fought under the Colonel in the Congo). Mike reassured me during lunch that all the indications were very positive and that the outcome would be good, but it would take time and the more time that passed by, the better it would be. He also said the people of the Seychelles where island people, who depended largely on tourism and were at heart a loving type of people. The worry though, was the Russians and Tanzanians who were on the island. Mike explained that the mercenaries who had returned on the Air India plane would have to be tried for hijacking and this could in its own way help to facilitate the release of the six mercenaries left behind on the Seychelles. I came back from the lunch feeling much more positive and as I drove home, I was suddenly overcome with a lot of mixed feelings, a mixture of relief and yet sadness, because more time was going to be needed, a lot more time, and it had taken such a long time already.

During this time I formed a deep friendship with Karen Dalgleish who was my main contact with the rest of the mercenary group. A meeting was arranged for all the wives and families of the group who were on the Seychelles, to meet with the attorney appointed by Mike Hoare to handle both the defence of the hijack group and our group on the Seychelles. We met at the Caisters Hotel on the Berea area of Durban, early one evening. There was a journalist there from the *Sunday Times* who suggested it would be a good idea for the wives and family to travel to the Seychelles for the trial, as this would create a good impression with the local people and the world press, making the mercenaries seem less like hardened criminals if they had the support of their families. He went on to say that it would be quiet safe, as we would have the protection of the press. I thought this was a brilliant idea, but found I was the only one to think so, as all the others seemed more apprehensive. When the attorney arrived I took one look at him and I thought of Count Dracula. There he was in his long following cloak, having just come from court and I was instantly struck by a sense of doom. The following Sunday we all met at Count Dracula's palatial beach house at La Lucia. He had hired the house in preparation for the trail of the hijackers in Pietermaritzburg. He kept us waiting for almost two hours, while his maid's little son careered around about us on a little tricycle. His first words to me were, 'Your husband is going to have to carry the death penalty, as like a race horse he will be judged on form, being a former Selous Scout and having been caught with his weapon there is no defence.'

With that I snapped, and replied, 'You Sir! Will not be representing my husband,' and I stormed out.

What had I done? How do I now go about arranging the defence? Let alone how will I be able to pay for it? I went back with Karen to the Riviera Hotel and it was here that Mike Hoare found me and listened to my reasoning. I felt that having Count Dracula defend Aubrey, would be like giving him the death penalty before the trial had even started. Mike said that he was now also having doubts that we had the right person defending the group on the island and we should change legal representation. I was both relieved and excited when Mike agreed and I then asked, 'Where to now?' Ken Dalgleish and his brother-in-law, Ian, were also present and it was suggested that we get the best Eastern bloc attorney to defend the men. Telephone calls were made, but the attorney we had set our sights on, was not available. It was then decided that a London based Queen's Counsel by the name of Nicholas Fairburn might be a good bet. I was not familiar with his name, so I just went along with what was decided. It seems I was not the only one who was not happy with Count Dracula, as at the same time the mercenaries who were on trial for the hijacking were also feeling he was not the person they wanted to defend them and they too changed attorneys. This then caused a split in the ranks with what had been a joint defence for the hijacking trial.

The wives and families of the prisoners on the island were asked to get a change of clothes for their husbands as these would be needed for the trail. This was quiet a mission as we had no idea how much weight they had lost and what condition they were in. After great deliberation, I chose a light grey three-piece suit, white shirt, red tie, and really soft black leather shoes. These were put into a suitcase and taken over to the island by the team of attorneys (at this point we were still to meet the defence team).

So it came to pass that we, the wives and families of the guys on the island, were asked to go to the Elangeni Hotel to meet with Nicholas Fairburn (the night prior to him leaving for the Seychelles). At this meeting we met our Durban based attorneys Graham Fowlis and Jeremy Ridl. My first impression of Nicholas was that he had just come straight out of a Charles Dickens novel, complete with fob watch, chain and glasses. He was very upbeat and agreed that it would create a good impression if the wives and families could be there for the trial.

There was a very humorous event later on in the evening, after the meeting. We (the ladies) went down stairs to discuss what we thought of Nicholas, Graham and Jeremy as this was the first time we had met them. We were all most impressed and quiet happy with the change. We met in the bar 'Churchill's'; this was downstairs from where the meeting had been held. When we went to order our drinks at the bar (we were sitting in an alcove, just off the bar area), there was a group of guys drinking at the bar and they tried to pick us up. We just ignored them. They then said, 'We must be nice and feel sorry for them, as they were part of the mercenary group who were to be tried for hijacking and that they needed some understanding.' This we knew was untrue and the remark was greeted with loud laughter from us all. I have often wondered what they would have felt like, if they were to have known whom they were talking to. We discussed going to the Seychelles and it seemed that I was alone in my thinking, saying that I would like to go; the others were quite frankly too afraid. I then went about making plans. How on earth could I make this happen?

I then remembered the journalist who was present at the Caisters. He was from the *Sunday Times* – Alan Joseph I think his name was. Anyway with the help of Karen and Ken, I contacted Alan. He listened to me and said he would see what he could do. He later said that he was unable to arrange anything through the *Sunday Times*, but had found out that the *Rapport* newspaper would jump at the idea. They had already taken Ina Dolinchek, the wife of Martin Dolinchek, over to the islands a few weeks previously. By now Martin had already decided that he was to be defended independently from the rest of the group. Ina too had decided the one trip was enough and did not want to repeat the experience. I thought that the offer was a great idea and that this would really suit me. The *Rapport* was an Afrikaans newspaper and with everyone I knew being English speaking, it was highly unlikely that they would read a lot of what I had to say. The newspaper had agreed to pay for my return flight to the Seychelles and my hotel accommodation. It was great.

I organised for the boys to be looked after by some really great friends (Kish and Viv Probert) and before I knew it, I was on a flight to Johannesburg en route to the Seychelles. The morning before I flew out, I met with Eddie Botha the journalist from *Rapport*, and a photographer. Many photos were taken and a short story was written. Eddie then said it would be better for us not to sit next to each other on the aircraft, as all the journalists knew I would be flying out in this way, but by being separated I may escape being noticed. This was not to be; it was as if I had a big sign over my head telling the world who I was and immediately after take-off I was completely surrounded. The men sitting in the seat next to me informed me they were from the Seychelles and that they fully supported the coup. They were escorting the body of a dead relative (who had passed away peacefully in South Africa) back to the Seychelles. This made me feel a little uneasy, as I was already nervous enough wondering what lay ahead for me once we had passed through the airport. On my arrival, I was greeted as if I were any ordinary visitor. It was after I had cleared through immigration that I realised my purse was missing; I did not have much in it, but it did upset me. The airport officials where fantastic and they even arranged for a search of the aircraft, but the purse was never found. Who had taken it? It could be anyone's guess. It could have been the guys sitting next to me or one of the many journalists asking questions. I put this behind me and I eventually boarded the bus which was to take us to the hotel.

My first impression of the Seychelles was one of absolute amazement. How could this be happening in such a beautiful part of the world? The climate is hot (just like a typical Durban summer's day), the sky blue, the ocean bluer and the sand was white, just like talc powder. The hotel which I was booked into was oddly enough the same hotel as Aubrey had been in prior to the failed coup. The hotel was built in an open plan style with the downstairs bar area and restaurant not fully walled; it was built like this in order to allow what breeze there was, to gently cool the area. It really looked fantastic.

My first instinct was to see Aubrey, but our legal team informed me this was not possible, so the Sunday after we arrived was spent travelling around the island, with

Eddie and I getting to know each other. It was decided that during this difficult time, Eddie would observe what happened each day, but would not necessarily report on each incident. Each Friday he would put on a tape recorder and ask me a series of questions (some of which he would have already known the answers to) and if I answered and it was on the tape, he would then publish whatever was said. I thought this a really great arrangement. Eddie gave me some really good advice: I should not wear sunglasses – as if I was photographed it would look like I had something to hide; I should not be photographed with a glass in my hand, even if it was water – this could be misconstrued as being an alcoholic drink; likewise I was to avoid having a photo taken whilst smoking (this was hard, as by this stage I was almost a chain smoker). As for the rest of the journalists, when they discovered I was contracted to the *Rapport* newspaper the heat was off and they then did not try to interview me, but would of course report on anything they witnessed.

The day of the trial arrived, and this was to be held at the Mason du Peuple, a building that resembled an old castle. This was to be my first sight of Aubrey. We arrived early and waited for the military truck to arrive. Aubs got out handcuffed to Martin Dolinchek and we briefly kissed hallo.

'What happened to you?' he asked. 'You look like a bag of bones.' (I had lost a lot of weight in the preceding months; prior to this my nickname had been 'Chubby Chops' which alluded to my weight. It was then that I was rechristened 'Bones'.)

The police took me up the narrow stone steps to the mezzanine floor. It was like something out of the movies. Below and directly in front of us sat Aubs and the rest of the group. They were handcuffed to a railing in front of where they sat. To the left sat the judge, a Jamaican, Justice Earl Seaton. He appeared to be an enormous man. He was dressed in a long flowing red robe and a wearing a large white wig. Facing him sat the legal teams, all dressed in black gowns and also wearing white wigs. On the opposite side, level to me, above the group on trial, sat members of the press and a diminutive grey haired lady, Mrs Turner, who had come to try and get Martin Dolinchek to admit to murdering her son on behalf of the apartheid government. I sat trying to talk to Aubrey through my eyes. He was looking better that I thought he would, thin, but the suit I had sent over for the trail did fit him nicely.

I found it difficult to concentrate on what was happening. It seemed so unreal. How could this be happening? This sort of thing only happens in the movies. All of a sudden I heard the Judge saying we would break and come back in the morning and he cautioned that no one except the legal team would have access to the accused. I went downstairs to say goodbye to Aubs. I was waiting just inside the passage with all the press; most of the onlookers had already gone outside for a better view. As Aubs, who was now handcuffed to Barney came to go past me, I reached forward to kiss him goodbye. With that a large guard grabbed me and pushed me to the floor, saying that contact with the accused was forbidden. Aubs jerked forward to hit the guard and I shouted, 'It's alright. I'm OK.'

Barney quickly pulled him back saying to him, 'Don't do anything stupid.'

I got up from the floor and watched them being led away. As the truck drove away, I was very upset; my emotions had gone all over the place. Firstly I had seen Aubrey which was terrific and the next thing I was being flung to the ground. I was very quiet as we returned to the hotel. We had not long been back at the hotel when I got a phone call from the Police to say I must report to the police station.

Eddie drove me down to the police headquarters; he was very worried at what might happen. What could this mean? On arrival I was asked to go into the Police Commissioner's office. Eddie waited outside. This was my first meeting with James Pillay the Commissioner of Police. I immediately sensed this was someone I could trust. He apologised for the behaviour of the guard at the court and he told me that permission had been granted for me to visit Aubrey at the prison. I was so excited. I hurriedly got into the car with his second in command, Deputy Commissioner Max Fontaine and we drove towards the prison, which was an army camp that overlooked the harbour; it was a short distance from the town. We got to the first boom gate and at this point the soldiers on duty had a heated discussion with Max Fontaine. They would not let us proceed, so we returned to the Police Station. Several phone calls were made in heated Creole; I could not understand anything. We then got back into the car and drove once again to the camp. This time they reluctantly let us pass; however, a soldier quickly got in to the car and seated himself next to me. He had his AK 47 off safe, and he stared menacingly at me. I started to get rather scared. The car came to a stop and I was escorted into the building and up some stairs to the Camp Commandant's office. The Major sat at his desk and asked me to come in and sit. This was my first meeting with Major Marengo. He was a rather short man who seemed to be brisling with antagonism. It was clear he did not approve of this meeting. I sat there trying to be polite. Aubrey was eventually shown in and we sat next to each other holding hands. Now that I was closer, I could see how thin he was and when I looked at his hands, it was as if I could see right through his skin; he was so pale, I could clearly see all the veins. We sat not knowing what to say. There was so much to say, but how? Aubs asked after the boys and I explained to him that they were staying with very good friends of ours. After about five minutes Marengo said that it was enough and that I must now leave. We had not had any time together. I left feeling so upset and emotional. I was taken back to the Police station, where James Pillay spoke to me and apologised for the short visit and he said that he would see what he could do for me regarding future visits. For my own protection from any radical elements that may be on the island, he had assigned undercover officers to protect me. I was not sure how I felt, but thanked him anyway. Meanwhile there was Eddie, totally frantic for he had no idea what had happened. He suspected the worst and he thought that I must have been arrested or some other dreadful thing had happened. He was both relieved and really amazed to hear my story.

The following day we were back at court again, but I did not try to greet Aubs. I just hung back from the crowd, which made the entire journalist corps curious. Nicholas came over and out of the blue he said, 'Good news it's a boy.' I thought he had gone nuts, and then I realised Princess Di must have had her baby and that it was a boy.

It was strange to think of how the British aristocracy had importance even here at this time (over the next few weeks I was given the nickname 'Lady Di of the Islands'). At the tea recess, I joined Aubrey and the group, along with our legal team in an office downstairs and now we had some time to talk. It was decided during that meeting that the group would plead guilty, as if they agreed to this, they were told that the charges against Susan Ingle would be dropped and that she would be sent home. I was not too happy with this decision; however, Nicholas said he was sure that they would never be able to make the charge of high treason stick, particularly as they were all non-nationals. Back in court Nicholas argued their case until lunchtime. He was rather brilliant. He said that it was like charging a person for rape, when all they had done was park on a yellow line. During the lunch break the group was sent back to the prison. I joined the legal team and the world press at the 'Pirate Arms', a well-known restaurant quite near the court. I watched with some concern as Nicholas Fairburn who was holding court with the world press, was downing double gin and tonics as if there was no tomorrow. I wanted to say something, but of course I did not.

After lunch we went back into court again and it was announced that the group with the exception of Martin Dolinchek, would plead guilty; this meant that effectively, their trial was now over. Susan went home that day and the trail was to now continue the next day for Martin Dolinchek. The rest of the group would have to wait until this trial of Martin's was over.

Life took an unreal turn. Here we were on this beautiful holiday resort, with nothing to do but wait for Dolinchek's trial to be completed. The world press is a strange lot. One day while a group of journalists and myself where relaxing at the hotel, one of the journalists kept saying he had to speak to me. I found this strange, as they generally left me alone (due to my contract with *Rapport*). Eventually, I agreed to talk to him and we wandered off to the beach. It was here that he explained to me, that he was not only a journalist, but that he also worked for the CIA and that he wanted to let me know the details of the operation. He explained in great detail why the coup was necessary, being of strategic importance to the West, for the satellite tracking station and bunkering rights for the Western world's naval ships. He drew diagrams in the sand to explain everything. He asked me not to say anything to anyone and later that night he flew off the island (for a posting in the Middle East, I believe).

Dolinchek's trail took six weeks, and during this period I was able to see Aubrey about three times a week. Over a period of time Aubrey and I had become friends with Major Marengo and the visits would last a couple of hours, as by now we used to include the Major in our conversations. The normal procedure for the visit was that I would wait for a phone call from the Major, and he would tell me where I was to be collected from and more often than not he would collect me in his dark green Mercedes (with a toy gorilla dangling from the rear view mirror). If he himself could not collect me, he would send one of the lieutenants. It was during one of these chats, that we discovered that the original coup had also been launched from

Durban and there were numerous similarities to the present coup attempt. I even helped the Major pick out his lounge suite from a catalogue he had from Makro (a large department store) in Durban. It was clear he did not trust the police force and liked to work independently of them. Eddie was always nervous of these meetings as he felt that anything could go wrong. I was just happy that I was able to visit Aubs.

The rest of the time, I ended up acting like a typical tourist. My cover as far as the normal hotel guests where concerned, was that I was Eddie's secretary and he was reporting on the trial. We drove all over the island in a Mini Moke. What was amazing was to see how the temperature changed, when you went up into the mountains and travelled through the lush green plantations of tea and coffee.

Over the next six weeks, people tended to come and go in about a two-week cycle. I met three very special people during that period, two of whom I still correspond with today. Karen was a rotary exchange student on a visit, Liz was a divorcee who had just come on holiday to get over her divorce and Nellie who was from the Seychelles, was out on a visit from Australia. Nellie was a real character, she was a lady of the night in Australia and could she tell some wild stories. It was good to have a friend to talk to and to laugh with. It was also very nice not being afraid that the person you were talking to would just run off and print all that you have just said in the world press.

Then one day I was wandering around a Christian bookstore and could not believe my eyes when I bumped into a friend of my Mom and Dad from the Rhodesia days, Pam Mills. Roy, Pam's husband was working for an insurance company on the Seychelles. Karen and I then went to meet them for lunch; there, they were so shocked to discover the real reason as to why I was on the island. However, they were very supportive (in the months to come they were to play an import part in my life during the Seychelles affair).

As the weeks dragged on the *Rapport* newspaper recalled Eddie and I was informed that they could no longer keep paying for my accommodation. I understood this and was very grateful for all they had already done for me. The hotel heard about this and they were fantastic in agreeing to pay for the remainder of my stay. James Pillay arranged for the funds that had been confiscated from Aubrey at the time of his arrest to be transferred to me. It was a continual source of amazement to me how wonderful everyone was. Many a time whilst I was shopping in Victoria, I would walk into a shop to buy washing powder or goodies for Aubs, when the owner of the shop would give me gifts and let me know that we had their full support. They often gave gifts such as a sarong for me, beach towels for the boys, and sweets and biscuits for me to take to Aubrey. Despite the worries of the James Pillay, I very seldom felt afraid of these loving people. With Eddie's departure I was now truly alone. However, a large contingent of journalists had remained and of course there was our legal team (which included a local attorney Kieran Shah), so I knew that it would be all right.

Kieran Shah, who looked to be of Indian origin, was a tall and slender man, a very nice person, and he had taken on the case at the time of the men's arrest. He proved to be wonderful in many ways, taking care of the men as best he could. He worked out of small rooms, on the top floor of a ramshackle double storied building. It was evident he was not a wealthy attorney; I often wonder how successful he became after such a high profile case, and I really hope that he has done well.

Then one day I was asked to meet the Major just on lunchtime. He seemed in a very jubilant mood as we drove up to the army camp. He told me that he had a real treat for me: I was to have lunch with my husband. On arrival at the barracks, instead of going into the Major's office, which is where we normally met, I was shown through the gate into the prison. I had a rather unnerving feeling when the gate slammed shut behind me. Still feeling nervous, I was taken into the old waiting room in the centre of the prison. Aubrey was already there; he was also looking fairly unsure of what to expect. Once we were seated, Bobby Sims arrived and acting as if he were the *maître d'* in a five star restaurant (complete with a dish cloth draped over his arm) he served me a cup of water as if it were a fine wine. Then he quietly shuffled off and left us to our meal. It was rather surreal. I am not too sure that this kind gesture would ever be repeated too many times anywhere else in the world. Aubs and I were served the normal meal that all the prisoners had; this consisted of fish and rice. The fish was served complete with eyes, scales and bones, all floating in a thin tomato and onion gravy. It did not look too appetizing, but I did not want to offend anyone, so I cheerfully and slowly, nibbled away at it, hoping that no one would notice that I was having difficulty in eating the meal. The luncheon lasted for about an hour and then I was taken back to the Major's office, where I thanked him. I was then taken down to the vehicle for the return journey to my hotel. It was a wonderful thing that the Major had done; it is a moment that I will never forget.

When I returned to the hotel I was so excited that I told the legal team what had happened. It puzzled me that they were not impressed. I later found out Nicolas Fairburn had given the *Scope* (a South African magazine) an exclusive on the lunch; in his version, which was later published, he used a lot of poetic license that also included somewhere in the release, the use of a silver candelabra etc. The *Scope* team had come out to the Seychelles with the blessing of our legal team as they were assisting us in trying to raise funds for the men's defence and part of this was done by selling exclusives to the magazine. However the *Scope* team had only stayed one week and in that time they could not get used to the way they were kept under constant surveillance and had their room searched whenever they went out. By now I had got used to this, and had come to accept it as normal practice.

Suddenly and out of the blue, Fairburn became insistent that I should leave the island, which of course I refused; I could see no reason why I should leave. Fairburn entirely on his own bat had also let it be known to the police and subsequently to the majors that I would be leaving.

The following morning I received a phone call from Major Marengo; he was clearly in a very upset frame of mind. He arranged for me to meet outside the milk depot and he himself came to collect me. He did not say a word on the drive up to the army barracks, but once inside his office he started ranting and raving that he was offended, that following his kindness to me (the luncheon), I had repaid him by wanting to just leave the island. Things became rather heated, when suddenly, I came to my senses. Here I was, shouting back at him, pounding his desk; this really was a bizarre state of affairs. I, as a prisoner's wife should not be shouting and acting in this manner. Eventually things calmed down and I got him to believe that I had no intention of leaving. It was a very unpleasant experience and I do not think I was even allowed to see Aubrey that day.

After a very long and protracted period Dolinchek's trial finally ended and that also meant that all the men had to be at the court once again. We met in a small side room, just before going into the main court. The attorneys Graham, Kieran and Nicholas said that they felt that there would be an adjournment that day and that the following day or even after the weekend the sentences would be passed.

I went up to the mezzanine floor. James Pillay had already arranged for a lady police officer to be with me. I sat facing the men below. Things seem to happen so quickly. Before I knew it Aubs (who was the first to be called) was asked to stand and the judge read out the various charges from the charge sheet and swiftly moving on, he then the pronounced the guilty verdict. With that Aubs was asked if he had anything to say, Aubs said he was sorry for the heartache he had caused to his family and everyone else. When Aub had finished we were all expecting the rest of the men to be given their verdicts, but no, suddenly and without warning, the judge then pronounced the death sentence.

'Frank Brooks you will be put to death in a manner so decided by…' His voice seemed to trail on and on…

Because it had happened so quickly, it came as a shock to all of us. I just kept looking straight at Aubs whilst I held the police officer's hand. The first thoughts I had were: do not react, all the men are counting on you, and do not cry or do anything stupid. The blood was pounding in my head; all the press and everyone else in the courtroom had their eyes fixed on me. After what seemed an eternity all the men where finally sentenced. I left the court with Graham Fowlis and we drove straight to the hotel. We sat in the garden and Graham ordered a gin and tonic for each of us, along with a ham sandwich. We did not say a word. Suddenly it started to rain lightly and with that my tears started falling, but not for long. Graham was very supportive and he kept on repeating to me, this is not the end, there was still the appeal. That night Graham Fowlis arranged for us to go out to dinner. It was the very last thing I felt like, but one did have to put on a brave face. When I came downstairs to meet them, Nicholas Fairburn was there, bare footed, obviously having had one or two too many and clearly distraught. Would you believe it, we spent the entire evening consoling him.

In the morning when I awoke, the full impact of what had happened came crashing down on me. I did not want to face anyone, and spent the day crying and drinking Coca-Cola. The hotel staff just kept bringing me soft drinks; they knew I was terribly upset. I even refused to speak to anyone on the phone. As dusk fell there was a knocking coming from the hallway, and although I did not feel like it, I made my way to the door, opened it and to my surprise I found that the Catholic Bishop of the island had come to comfort me and give me support. He was a wonderful person, very kind and understanding. As we talked that day I learnt from him that his brother had been killed during the previous coup when President René took power. After about an hour he left and I did feel a lot better, much calmer and I think more prepared for what lay ahead.

The following morning James Pillay sent a car to collect me. Once I was in his office, he put on some music and started to speak in a very low tone. He told me that he could give me no proof but that I should believe him that the death sentence would never take place. He also said that I should go home to look after my two boys and that one day Aubs would come home. I believed him. I went to see Aubs during the day before I left; it was truly the hardest thing to do to say goodbye. I did however manage to tell him about my conversation with James Pillay. The time just sped by and before I knew it I was in a car driving back down the hill, full of mixed emotions and wondering what would really happen

The aircraft bound for Johannesburg left the Seychelles at about 3.00 am in the morning; also on board were the journalists, they too were now all returning home. By now we had all become good friends; they had in their own rough way, tried to be a comfort to me. There was one very tearful moment when Eugene Hugo produced photos, that until then I had never seen. They were of Aubrey shortly after his arrest, all beaten up; he had been shot, manacled and was lying on a cell floor. My mind then went into overtime, clinging to James's words and just praying they would be true. As the plane lifted off the ground my heart broke; it was just so very, very hard to leave.

On my return home no one would believe me when I said that one day Aubs would come home. I had no proof – I just knew it. I was unable to tell anyone about my meeting with James, so most people thought I was in denial. Everyone was most supportive at home, and at that time various world statesmen had made several pleas for clemency. The only one to make a plea in South Africa was Bishop Desmond Tutu; I will always remember him for this and I will also for ever hold him in high esteem.

The weeks, then months went by. Some crazy plots where hatched by the rest of the mercenaries on trial for the hijacking. One plot was that they would arrange for a fleet of yachts to sail into Mahé and rescue the men. This put fear in my heart as I felt that if they did try this and it went wrong, I was sure that the men that had already been sentenced to death, would surely be put to death

A few months passed and the Seychelles was back in the news. There had been another attempted coup. At home we had a very stressful few days wondering what was happening. Eventually our attorneys discovered that some of the military had staged a mutiny and had tried to have a number of the majors removed. But the men were safe. Later we were told that they had now all been transferred out of solitary confinement and had been placed into a communal cell.

I wrote to Aubrey every week but received only one or two letters in reply. I had some really exciting family news to tell him: his daughter Kathleen – who after

Aubs' divorce had been adopted by her mother and new husband, and therefore we had not seen or heard from her since she was about eleven years old – and her husband were living in Empageni, a town not too far from where we lived and it was wonderful to see what a lovely lady she had grown up to be. I wrote to Aubrey with great excitement.

One Thursday evening the boys and I were about to go off to the drive-in cinema to watch the film *E.T.* and we were all in the car and ready to leave, when I heard the phone ringing; something made me get out quickly and I ran to answer the phone. It was Aubs phoning from the president's office and at the request of the president he asked me to come to the Seychelles as soon as possible. I of course agreed and spent the night thinking of how I would be able to get there. Luckily *E.T.* amused the children. Early on the Friday morning I contacted Graham Fowlis to tell him the news; he agreed that I should go as soon as possible. Luckily my Dad had sent some money out to us the previous week to help tide me over while Aubs was away. I managed to get a flight the very next day. I contacted Roy and Pam Mills, the good friends of the family whom I had met in the book store during the trial, and asked if I could stay with them for the week. They were happy for me to stay and so the following morning I found myself on the way back to Johannesburg en route to the Seychelles. It was Saturday evening when I arrived. Roy and Pam were there to meet me and I must admit, this time around I was rather nervous, as unlike the last time, now there was no press protection and the only one who knew I was coming to the island was Kieran Shah the Seychellois attorney. On the Sunday morning I contacted Major Marengo and he agreed to let me see Aubs. It was wonderful to see Aubs again and he was certainly looking well, and much better than when I had last seen him. We had a long chat together with Major Marengo. I heard all about the attempted mutiny and how their previous prison warders were now in the cells that Aubs and the others had been held in after the coup attempt. The old laundry had now been converted into a communal cell. Aubs was not too happy with this arrangement and said he preferred to be in solitary, as the communal cell was not bringing out the best in the others.

It was a very strange week. Every morning Roy would have a full English breakfast whilst listening to the BBC World News on the radio. Pam and I kept to eating our yogurt and fruit. But it did bring a smile to me whenever it was time for Roy to leave for work; it was almost as if he were still living in the UK, as he would hurry off complete with umbrella and bowler hat. This was all happening in the tropical heat of the Seychelles. It was very unusual to say the least. I met with Aubs every day, along with the Major. The message from President René was very clear: it appeared that he was just waiting for the opportune time to release the men, but apparently the South African government were not too happy with this arrangement and kept putting stumbling blocks in the way of process. Through Major Marengo, I was asked if I could speak to the South African government in order to try and hasten the negotiations regarding the release. What they asked me to do, however, was to convince all the parties involved, that their 'Leave to Appeal' should be dropped; this worried me somewhat. It did appear that the Seychelles government were sincere, but again I had no proof. Would I be able to do this without anything concrete to back me up? The other worry was that now I was no longer in tourist mode on the Seychelles, how were the locals going to treat me? I should never have worried, because I was spoken to on several occasions by a lot of the locals who were always very open and friendly. They also expressed how disappointed they were that the coup Aubs was involved in had failed. I learnt about the youth camps: I was told that once the children were old enough to leave school, they had to go away to a youth camp on one of the islands, and if they did not do this they were unable to gain work on the Seychelles; this displeased the older people as they felt the children were being indoctrinated. All too soon the week had passed and I once more had the heart-wrenching ordeal of leaving Aubs and returning again to South Africa. On the journey home I did some real soul-searching. I was trying to sort out how best to approach the task that lay ahead, trying to find a way to carry out the wishes of the Seychelles government in order to obtain the release of Aubs and the men. It must be also remembered that the government in South Africa at that time, was the old Afrikaans apartheid regime. In the country at that time a woman had little or no standing and here I was a woman, and an English-speaking woman at that. This surely would carry very little weight; how would they respond to what I had to say? I was excited, but at the same time unsure and nervous of what lay ahead.

Upon my return I immediately went to visit Graham Fowlis and told him the story. He was not too happy about my feelings regarding the dropping of the appeal. He said he would make some enquiries as to whom I could speak with, regarding the government's tardiness in obtaining the release of the men. I duly found myself once again sitting in an aircraft; this time I was flying off to a meeting in Pretoria. I was met at the airport by the mother of one of the mercenaries who had come back on the Air India plane (he was a member of the recces) and her husband (he was somehow connected with the South African government). I was taken to the government buildings in Pretoria and upon arrival I was ushered into a small room in which there were three men (I cannot remember their names and I am not sure if I was ever told who they were, or which department they had come from). I spent an agonizing five hours being questioned over and over again. They knew everything about me and also everything about anyone I was associated with; it was frightening, no, terrifying. The men were convinced I had now become a communist and that somehow I had been brain washed by the Seychelles government (in that era the security authorities thought there was a communist behind every tree). Eventually I was allowed to leave, but not before being threatened.

'Do not, let anyone know of this meeting, especially the press,' they growled at me. By now I was even questioning my own sanity; I was not sure who I was, or even where I was. I was completely shell shocked; if I was afraid before, now I was terrorised. I did not know who to trust and I knew my every move was being watched.

The one thing that I did get done was that after a meeting with the other wives and the attorneys the Leave to Appeal was dropped. This gave me nightmares, as I was so afraid that perhaps the South Africans where correct; that maybe I had been brain washed and my trust in the Seychelles was misplaced.

Weeks turned into months and still no news. Letters were infrequent. I met with the British Ambassador in the Seychelles and as I am a British subject (and a couple of the other mercenaries were also British) he obtained permission for me to pay visits to Aubs and the other guys, and every now and then I would get an update. I also telephoned Major Marengo several times just to find out how Aubs was and this small amount of contact that I had was of great comfort to me.

Then all of a sudden without warning the men were moved off Mahé to Isle de Platte, a small island many miles away from the main island. What could this mean? I telephoned the Major who assured me that this was a good sign and that I should just be patient. I was alarmed at the possibility of something going wrong, especially now that there was no one keeping watch, no British Ambassador, no attorneys and no press. What if they just disappeared? They were sentenced to death after all. Eventually I was told that these things take time, perhaps even years and years. I clung to my trust and faith that they would one day return. On one occasion the British Ambassador managed to visit the men. He sent me a photograph of Aubs looking tanned healthy and very fit. When I first saw the photograph I did not know who it was; I did not recognise him and when I did, it made me feel much better.

The news of their pending return happened just as suddenly. I caught a news bulletin on the radio saying it was reported from London that the men were soon to be released and that they were to be sent home. I went through the normal motions phoning everyone, the attorneys, Major Marengo, the press. We had by now had a number of false alarms, so I was very sceptical. I pieced together the events. Apparently, a British newspaper the *Mail on Sunday* had visited the men on Isle de Platte and they were told that the men were due to fly back to Mahé on the Thursday night. The following day I sat glued to the radio with my friend Peggy; we were playing scrabble to pass the time. Then came the long awaited news broadcast, announcing that the men would be returning on the Saturday. At the same moment I got a phone call from the *Sunday Times* newspaper telling me the news and asking for a reaction; my first reaction was: how can I get to Johannesburg to meet the plane? The *Sunday Times* newspaper was fantastic they took care of everything and in return I had to give them an exclusive story on Aubs' return. Roy (my youngest son) and I flew to Johannesburg that night and we were put up at the Carlton Hotel; the press even arranged for my hair to be done at 10 pm that night. Our other son Rory was already working and living in Johannesburg, but I could not make contact with him; I just had to hope that he would hear the news via radio or television and make contact with us.

We got to the airport before 5.00 am in the morning. A few of the other wives were there. I was very tense, as the plane was already over three hours late. Could this all be happening? Could this nightmare finally be coming to an end? We were all shown into a little room just inside the arrivals hall and then suddenly there was Aubs; it seemed so unbelievable. When we walked back out into the arrivals hall, there were hundreds of well-wishers and the people were shouting and cheering; it was so overwhelming. Luckily the reporters of the *Times* guided us through the crowd and out of the mayhem. Back at the hotel we sipped champagne and spoke. There was so much to say, and it was so strange. Eventually, the press left us. Aubs then wanted a hot bath, as the men had only had cold water for the past few years and when it was ready he climbed in clothes and all. It was winter and so very cold, but Aubs was so jubilant he did not feel cold at all. We made our way to the home of our good friends Kish and Viv Probert. They had been so amazing throughout the whole ordeal with us: all the fetching and carrying of me to and from the airport, looking after Roy and generally being so fantastic. We had a memorable braai and then the following morning we flew back to Durban. It was not all over though and it was certainly not a happy ever after event. I was still trying to hold down a job, and Barney and Aubs were always together. Sandra, Barney's wife had divorced him before Barney's return. Barney seemed to just move in and most of their days were spent in the pub. This was very hard on me as I never forgot the men in Pretoria and I was certain they would still be watching, which they were.

Barney and Aubs came back home one evening with a stranger. I was called from the kitchen and told that person wanted to talk to me. I was rather annoyed as I was busy trying to cook the supper. The guy sat there and said that Barney and Aubs had better stop talking about the whole affair. Barney and Aubs just laughed. Then he said pointing to me, 'You see your wife, she is in good health now, and I only hope she stays that way. Unless you stop talking, an accident may happen.' My blood ran cold; we had already heard of incidents happening to some of the other guys who had come back on the Air India flight. Two had died very mysteriously.

With that both Aubrey and Barney got extremely annoyed and told the person to leave immediately; he was quickly hustled out. After that night Aubs and Barney had a big change of attitude. We tried everything to find out who that person was. Was he military intelligence, special branch or the secret service? Each blamed the other. Life has never been the same since; the phone was always tapped from then on and whenever there was an incident or a meeting with someone who 'they' were watching or even a small hic-up somewhere else in Africa, we became the centre of attention once again. We were to be kept under continual surveillance for many years after that, even when there was a change in the government of South Africa.

Was it worth it? Personally, I discovered my strengths and realised that I was diplomatic even in the hardest of situations, but I did find it very difficult to talk to people for a long time afterwards; you just never knew who was listening. On the Seychelles, the Americans where given permission to use the satellite tracking station and the American and British fleet are able to use the harbour in Mahé. South African Airways have landing rights. It has been an experience and in retrospect I am glad that I have gone through it, but I would not like to go through it again.

Diane Brooks in South Africa

Diane Brooks awaiting news back home

British High Commission
Victoria House PO Box 161 Victoria Mahe Seychelles

Telex 269 (a/b UKREP SZ)
Telephone 23055/6

Mrs D L Brooks
74 Zulweni Gardens
Old Main Road
Amanzimtoti
4125
Natal

Your reference

Our reference
CON 384/2
Date
25 May 1983

Dear Mrs Brooks,

You will by now have heard that I was able to pay a visit to the captured mercenaries on Platte Island on 18 May 1983. I was fortunate enough to be able to take some photographs whilst I was there. I am enclosing a copy of one of these. The group are fit and well have become actively involved in shell collecting from the beautiful reef which surrounds the island and are making the best of conditions in their isolated home.

Yours sincerely,

Graeme Thomas

G G THOMAS

Letter to Di from the British High Commissioner

17
The Readjustment

A lot of people say they have difficulty readjusting to civilian life after war. I had to adjust after almost two years on death row. It is amazing how many of the small things in everyday life change over a period of two and a half years. Shortly after we arrived home, the first time I went into the bathroom to brush my teeth, I could not find the toothpaste tube. The more I asked Di where it was and the more she told me where to find it, the more confused I became, until she finally came and put it in my hand; it was toothpaste in a dispenser. I had never seen a dispenser like that that before. What was the world coming to? I remember walking around the supermarket a few days later and coming across these very small ovens; I could not fathom out who would want an oven that tiny. What could you possibly cook in it? A single roast maybe? I was still wondering about this, when one of the sales assistants who had obviously seen me with a puzzled look on my face came over and pointed out to me that it was a mini oven for baking bread. The Falklands War had happened in our absence and to make things a little bit more confusing for an avid sportsman, nearly all our local and international sports teams were full of new faces; the starting line up in the Grand Prix races also looked very different. On arrival at the airport in Durban I was told not to drive my car for a few days, as it was felt that I would have to first get used being amongst large groups of people and of course the traffic. However I had already decided that I was going to get on with my life the minute I returned, so at the airport I insisted on driving myself home, much to the annoyance of everyone else and especially those who only had my best interest at heart. Those first few weeks were full of many strange and exciting discoveries and I had also developed a new and rather bad habit: I could not walk past the fridge without opening it and devouring whatever was inside. Di spoke to our doctor about this and he told her not to worry; he said I would eventually get back to my normal eating habits, but for a while it was sweets, chocolates, ice creams, steaks and our favourite roasts. However, on the down side I had come back to find that my partner in the business had pulled out and let the business close. Di by now was working in real estate and was doing exceptionally well; this meant that she was working very long hours and weekends as well. Her boss and workmates were fantastic and she was very happy there. I did not handle this part of my return very well. In fact, in retrospect I handled it very badly. I think largely because I felt inadequate and mainly because I was not providing for our family. I probably resented her success and I made life very unpleasant for her at work, and eventually she found it easier to leave the job she enjoyed so much, in order to keep the peace with me, very sad but true. She had worked so hard to make sure that I had a good home to come back to and I had acted in this way. I did not know it at the time, but I was very mean and self-centred; it would be a very long time before I would realise this. I am not proud of the way I behaved when I first came back and truly regret it to this day. It proves once again that hindsight is certainly 20/20 vision.

Apart from messing up Di's career and a few other minor wobbles it was a fairly easy adjustment. The main difficulty is the way you just cannot believe your good fortune and that you actually survived. Back in Durban, I came to appreciate all kinds of things I might have taken for granted before: my family, especially Di, Rory, Roy, Kathleen and our wonderful grandchildren Toni, Tanya, Tara and Trey, and of course our many friends; the chance to earn a living; the wonderful climate; and the natural beauty around me. Freedom now has a very special meaning for me. I was also amazed at the way people seemed to welcome me back; people I did not know would walk up to me in the street to congratulate me, recognising me from television and the massive news coverage that had been generated. All kinds of new avenues seemed to just open up.

Colonel Mike Hoare was finally released from prison and we had a wonderful reunion in Hilton, a town just outside Durban in the province of Kwazulu Natal. He also left South Africa and moved to France where he continued to write books. He is an amazing man who has done so much good, especially in the Congo days when nuns and civilians were being beaten, raped, and killed on a daily basis. He led his men under very difficult circumstances in order to alleviate their suffering. How quickly the world forgets. I will always have the greatest respect and admiration for this remarkable man.

I got into the private security industry, specializing in protecting businesses against industrial espionage. It seemed natural after my military experience, and it was only once I had got involved that I realised what a vast and murky field this is. Everyone seems to be at risk of getting their trade and manufacturing secrets pinched, and it kept me very busy. I also got heavily involved in events management, organising all kinds of events on the Durban beachfront, including big events such as Vodacom Beach Africa (one of the biggest beach festivals in the world that included an international surfing competition). I ended up organizing the Durban leg of the Clipper Round-the-World Yacht Race, the South African national Jet Ski championships, the A1 Grand Prix (a street race in Durban) and many more international events.

The odd thing is that the political parties also showed an interest in me. As I have explained elsewhere in this book, my experience had very much modified my political views, from the simple them and us attitudes that I had in Rhodesia and South Africa. President René had shown me not just greatness of heart, he had shown me that socialism and communism is not necessarily the same thing.

Archbishop Tutu had been influential in getting our pardon and release. What had the apartheid government done for me? Absolutely nothing (that we were aware of) and I was aware now that race was an absolute political red herring.

You would have thought that a man who had been involved in a violent coup attempt would be shunned by the mainstream political parties, but this was not so. I was approached to run for parliament by three parties: the Democrats (who were very liberal), the Conservatives (who wanted a return to Verwoerd-style apartheid) and the Nationalists (Nats), who were then still in power and dismantling apartheid as fast as they could. I did not have much difficulty turning down the Conservatives but the Nats and the Democrats were both tempting options. In the end I steered clear of politics, on the very sound advice of Di's father. I was doing fine on my own, he told me. Politics would only distract me and hold me back. I am glad I followed his advice.

However, I did have one potentially very embarrassing experience with the far right wing. I used to, at times, conduct target-shooting exercises at the firing range in Amanzimtoti; this was mostly attended by normal civilians, their wives and families. The object of this training was to help them to become competent in using their own firearms for self-protection. However, the range would be hired out to various other groups as well. One day a certain individual on behalf of an un-named group had hired the range for the day, and I was asked to assist them as the range officer/instructor. I think it was my military background that got me roped in. The exercise was already well under way, when somebody came hurrying up to me in a bit of a flap and whispered to me that a huge Transvaal Vierkleur flag was flying at the gate. It turned out the shooting exercise was being held under the auspices of the Afrikaner Weerstandsbeweging (Afrikaner Resistance Movement also known as the AWB), a far-right paramilitary group that was threatening to take over the country by force.

This was just not on. I could not be part of it. It was like holding a shooting exercise in Ireland on behalf of the IRA. I called the organisers together and told them I would have to cancel the event unless they took down the flag. They were not too happy about it, but eventually agreed. I was relieved when that exercise ended.

So, I had had contact with the far right wing, the right wing and the centrist and liberal parties. Did I shun the ANC (African National Congress – Nelson Mandela's party)? Not at all. Once they were unbanned, they in fact approached me – not to run on their ticket but for some professional assistance.

Soon after being unbanned by FW de Klerk, the ANC held their first legal conference at the campus of the University of Durban-Westville; the university was on vacation at the time. The ANC delegates were there in their thousands, most of them staying in the vacant students' residences. The international media were there in their droves and the spooks of the world's intelligence agencies obviously were there as well, almost certainly including South African military intelligence, the security police and BOSS, who were then still controlled by the Nats.

I was approached by the ANC's head of security, Mo Shaik, to sweep the place for surveillance devices (de-bugging – counter-surveillance): the main conference hall, the committee rooms, the admin offices, everywhere. Why he chose me I cannot say. He knew very well that I had been a Selous Scout and Seychelles mercenary; that I was hardly an ANC sympathiser. But maybe he wanted somebody who was completely out of the loop, not connected with any political party or intelligence agency, or to any of the ANC's factions. I like to think it was my professional reputation in countering industrial espionage that swung it for me, for by now I was well known in the industry and in fact had become the President of the South African Council of Civil Investigators. At any rate, I was hired and the man who had been on death row for attempting to overthrow a leftist president was now working for the ANC.

Did I find any bugs? You bet I did and every time I went back to sweep again there seemed to be more. It was a fantastic way of getting new equipment for my company. A lot of people were keen to snoop on the ANC and it was quite a task keeping the place clean. The ANC seemed well pleased with what I did and they paid me without a murmur. I find this an amusing part of my CV: Aubrey Brooks the mercenary soldier, working for the ANC (they were very pleasant and professional people to work with as well).

The beachfront event managing began to snowball and we were asked among other things to help with the project management of the A1 Grand Prix, a motor race along the beach front of Durban; this was another amazing experience. Then, the black empowerment policies of the Durban City Council were put into place and this meant that only the black consortiums (the previously disadvantaged people) were getting the contracts; I understood the reasons for this approach, but at the same time I felt that a lot of good quality expertise was being lost. This was a time where skills transferal would have been a much better option. Although I thoroughly enjoyed working for and with the people of the city, I found it more difficult to deal with this growing marginalization and so we made plans to move overseas.

I relocated to the Isle of Man where Di has family; her Grandmother was born on the island and of course our four grandchildren are not far away in the UK. I have set up a similar event management business, dividing my time between writing and running motivational courses. Our two sons Rory and Roy, our daughter Kathleen and our four wonderful grandchildren Toni, Tanya, Tara and Trey all play a major part in our life (we have new additions to our family, Tanya and Michael presented us with, Taven, our first great grandchild and Tara followed suit with another great grandchild, Blake) and I could say that yes – life has been good.

For some of the others who were on the islands with me, freedom has not been so good. Barney Carey and I were as close as brothers; he had been such a staunch friend to whom I owe my life (after that hospital incident with the Tanzanian guards). Sadly he died in a Dar es Salaam hotel room a few years after our release; this was under the most mysterious of circumstances, almost certainly murder. He was involved in international arms dealing – quite above-board as I understand it – but the arms business is dirty and ruthless at all levels. He was discovered dead in his room, nothing had been stolen, thousands in foreign currency were found, American dollars, British pounds, German marks, etc. all untouched. His death has never been explained. Strange! However, I am sure that he is at peace now; rest well my pal. After completing this book I received an email out of the blue from Barney's son Nicky (from his first marriage). I have spoken with him and we are now in contact and are hoping to meet very soon – he has a lovely wife and a beautiful daughter. I cannot believe how much he looks like Barney (the resemblance is uncanny; they could have been twins). I am sure that Barney would be proud of them.

Jerry Puren, who was a lot older than the rest of us, died in Durban of natural causes. Bobby Sims is still somewhere in Pietermaritzburg, I think, but we never did have anything in common and I lost contact with him almost from the time we were released. Ken Dalgliesh came back into our lives for a short while and we tried to form a security company and also tried a number of other ventures, but it was never the same again, he only recently passed away in Durban. We are now also in contact with his wife Karen and their daughter Samantha.

Roger England returned to the United Kingdom. He was a loner who lived in a world of his own; he would sit alone and turn things over in his mind for hours on end. He was a good soldier and totally reliable, but nobody really got close to him. Just recently I have spoken with him and I must say how nice it was to establish contact again after all those years and we are planning to meet again soon.

Martin Dolinchek joined up with the ANC soon after we returned. I understand he crossed into Zimbabwe and from there made his way to Zambia. I suppose you cannot blame him when you consider the way his government disowned and dropped him, even though he was supposedly in the Seychelles on their behalf. They could have treated him better. I found the guy unstable and a total menace; the ANC are welcome to him. I believe he now has some sort of job with the National Intelligence Agency (which replaced BOSS) or the ANC, but I have no idea at what level or what he is doing. He phoned me once but apart from that I have had no contact.

Barney and I were as close as brothers. Roger was a loner, Jerry and Bobby had nothing in common with me. Ken and I had drifted apart and Martin was a complete crank. But we all had one thing in common: captivity. Four of us – Barney, Roger, Jerry and I – had a death sentence, under the shadow of which we lived for all that time. We will always remember that period of our lives.

The welcome home for Col. Hoare at Hilton in Kwazulu Natal.

18

The Selous Scouts

I have explained how my religious faith carried me through this ordeal. There was also the physical and mental side of it, and for that I have to thank my background in the Selous Scouts. If you could get through the selection ordeal, you could get through anything. Most applicants dropped out, some of them men already with excellent fighting records.

The Scouts were looking for something different, something special. We had to be able to survive in the bush, eating lizards, snakes, anything we could find. We had to endure extremes of fatigue, heat and thirst. Through all this we had to somehow keep our minds clear to achieve the objectives set for us. The training officers deliberately broke down the individual who came to them and then rebuilt him the way they wanted. But not everyone could cope; during the selection process they dropped out in their hundreds.

The Scouts were an outfit commanded by Lieutenant Colonel Ron Reid-Daly, who had served with the SAS in the highly successful campaign against communist insurgents in Malaya; he was a great leader of men and was justifiably proud of his unit, as we are of him. It was in Malaya that the SAS had out-guerrilla'd the guerrillas. Instead of allowing them the initiative by responding with more or less conventional infantry tactics, the SAS had become guerrillas themselves, mingling with the population, staying out in the jungle for weeks on end, becoming part of the local system and this paid off, thus giving the communists some very nasty surprises. They themselves were 'swimming among the people the way a fish swims in water' to quote Mao's *Little Red Book*. The operation in Malaya was probably one of the most successful in 'winning the hearts and minds'. The Americans were not to get anywhere near it in Vietnam.

In Rhodesia, the Selous Scouts operated much the same. Most of our troops were Africans, trained to exactly the same standards. They would mingle with villagers, even with ZANU and ZAPU guerrilla groups, wearing the East European camouflage outfits we always used in the operational zones and carrying AK 47s and other weaponry from the communist bloc. We would penetrate deep into Mozambique and other enemy-held territory and we sowed much mischief and division among the nationalist groups and their sympathisers. Also, we would guide our troops – usually carried by helicopter – into operations against bases that would not normally have been known without this type of operation; these were highly profitable in military terms and in boosting morale.

I have heard people say the Rhodesian Army was the best counterinsurgency force in the world at the time, and I like to think the Selous Scouts were right at the heart of it. Some of the things we did were a bit rough, I agree, but this was war and the nationalist terrorists were being even rougher. Besides, Rhodesia was fighting for survival. I like to think I am a moral person and not once did I have any misgiving about what we were doing in the Selous Scouts.

However, my real point is that life in the Scouts made us physically tough, resilient, and resourceful. You learned to use every little assistance nature gives you in the bush. It also gave us a mental toughness; we lived on our wits. We could be betrayed any minute and we knew what to expect if we were captured: the ZANU and ZAPU people were trained in communist interrogation methods. We could have ended up being interrogated by Chinese or North Koreans. We were trained to be ready for the kind of torture we could expect. We were also trained to give out just the dribs and drabs of information that were verifiably correct but of little consequence, and to keep the big story to ourselves. That is why when I was being beaten black and blue every day by a Tanzanian goon in the Seychelles, I was able to survive without cracking. I was not only physically tough, but mentally tough too. I gave out the bits of information that did not matter. I survive and I owe it to my training with the Selous Scouts.

I have carried this training into civilian life as well. I realise now that race simply does not matter; it is a decoy. Most of our Scouts were Africans and they were excellent fellows, the greatest buddies you could wish for. They were fighting the same war as us. They were ready to die for me and I was ready to die for them. When you are out in the bush surrounded by enemy, it does not matter a damn what the colour is of your buddy's skin, just so long as he does his bit to get you both out of the scrape.

There is also the loyalty. The Scouts' Shona motto *Pamwe Chete* means 'Together Only' or 'All Together' and we really do stick together, whether in combat while the war was still on or in the reunions that are held fairly regularly in South Africa. (I am told the Zimbabwean security services actually get a bit nervous when these functions are held and for no reason.) Loyalty to colleagues is another value that is well worth carrying forward into civilian life, and I like to think all we ex-Scouts do just that, rough and ready as some of us might otherwise be regarded.

I believe the code of the Selous Scouts was the epitome of the military values of manliness, courage, loyalty and devotion to duty. One day, when the propaganda and hysteria have died down and people look calmly and dispassionately at the facts, this outfit will be given the full recognition it deserves.

Selous Scouts cap badge

19
The Closing Chapter

No more 'funnies' for me. Apart from getting a bit old for this sort of thing, I have had more than my share of close shaves, taking into account the Bush War in Rhodesia as well. When you have been sentenced to death, then reprieved, there is a message: you need to get out and start doing the things in life that really count, like building something for your family; appreciating the beauty and wonder of the world you live in; and appreciating your family, friends, your fellow man, and your place in the universe.

I know I learned a lot from the Seychelles escapade. Most importantly of all, I learned that if you have faith in God, whoever you deem him to be, nothing can or will break you. I had rediscovered my faith. The Seychelles was a very tough lesson, and I regret that it caused such anguish for my wife, family and friends and this shows that even in adversity good can come about. The picture I mentioned earlier (of my wife and a young lady with a baby) was a picture of my daughter Kathleen from my first marriage; I had not seen her since she was twelve years old and the baby she was holding was our first grandchild, Toni. I am happy to say that she and all four of our grandchildren, Toni, Tanya, Tara and Trey play a very big part in our life today. The lessons learnt were immense and so valuable that all the suffering makes it worthwhile.

I discovered that things are not as simple and clear-cut as they might at first appear. People can talk about things like the communist threat – today it would be a different kind of threat, the war on terrorism – but this is often lazy talk; not too many people are prepared to get up and do something about it. The world is made up of different human beings and it is they who count.

I discovered that President René, who I had been programmed to detest for his socialism, is in fact a warm and highly principled human being to whom I owe my life. I probably will never fully support his political ideas but he is entitled to hold them. On our return Di and I telephoned him to thank him and a little later we received a signed photograph from him, wishing our family well for the future. We also received a Christmas card from the Commissioner of Police James Pillay.

Similarly, I had been programmed to detest people like Archbishop Desmond Tutu for his political activism, yet it was he who played a major role in securing a pardon for my comrades and me. What motive had he to intervene on behalf of what many would consider a bloodthirsty, freebooting mercenary who had once been in the forefront of the war against the forces of liberation in Zimbabwe? The only motive was his Christian forgiveness and compassion. As a professing spiritualist myself, I am humbled by it. I have subsequently been in contact with this great man and he has agreed to us meeting for a cup of coffee in the not too distant future.

I learned that the world is inhabited not by different races but by the human race. I had already begun to realise this in the Selous Scouts (that race was nonsense), but my experience with the gentle Seychellois people really brought it home in a hundred different ways. Left to their natural instincts, people are generally kind and considerate, whoever they might be.

I learned the value of true friendship, such as with Barney Carey who came back to look for me instead of taking the flight out of Mahé. I can only hope, that put to the test, I would do something similar.

Would I do it all again? It is a hypothetical question because the flesh is no longer as willing. But I suppose that hypothetically speaking, if I were given the opportunity to unseat a vicious usurper who was oppressing and brutalising his people, I would do it all again. But I hope that this time I would take the trouble to make sure the information was accurate and that I was not relying on the opinions of others. There are, and always will be shades of grey. Such a description certainly does not fit the now-retired President René, so in a sense was I wrong to set out to topple him? Who will ever know? All the objectives of what we had set out to do on that day back in November 1981 were ultimately achieved: the Americans had their satellite tracking station lease renewed, the South Africans had secured landing rights for their national carrier South African Airways, the bunkering facilities in Mahé were extended to the free world and I like to think that the people in the Seychelles may have ultimately benefited with President René having fresh look at his policies back home. I also firmly believe that I acted in good faith when I had set out on this mission. However, we do need to be aware of the political games that are continually being played out daily in all our lives.

The Seychelles experience – death row in paradise – has been for me like a cleansing fire that has left me with a new sense of wonderment at life itself. It has freed me from many kinds of distractions I had before. I now know it is my simple duty to live life to the full, and in doing so, serving my God and my fellow man. I can ask no more.

Appendix I

Extracts from *Armed Forces*, May 1977
The Selous Scouts

The Selous Scouts were a Special Forces unit of the Rhodesian Army that operated from 1973 until majority rule in 1980. They were named after the British explorer Frederick Courtney Selous (1851–1917). They were formed and commanded by Lt. Col. Ron Ried – Daly. They were acclaimed trackers, highly trained and accomplished in the art of counter insurgency warfare. This small unit was a highly effective fighting machine during the Rhodesian Bush War and there can be now doubt, that they were very successful in the fight against the Black Nationalist guerrillas of ZANLA/ZANU and ZIPRA/ZAP during this period of terror. The following is a report from a journalist who describes the selection process and is taken from an armed forces publication in May of 1977.

The advanced training base is about an hour's drive from Kariba, or a 30-minute boat trip on the edge of the famous man-made lake. It consists of a collection of grass-roofed huts, which, at first glance resemble a prisoner of war camp like those used by the Japanese in World War 11. The camp, known as the Wafa Wafa, takes its name from the Shona words Wafa Wasara, which loosely translated, means those who die, die - those who stay behind, stay behind. It is an appropriate motto - because the gruelling selection course here "kills off" more recruits than those who survive to finish successfully. That any of the recruits survive the training period at all seems a minor miracle, but they do and subsequently become the Rhodesian answer to terrorist infiltration. Principally they are taught to kill and survive and, in training, are pushed to their physical limits. Rations are cut to one sixth of that given to a man on normal active service. It is therefore appropriate to describe the grassy encampment as the selection and tracker-training headquarters of one of the most specialised and toughest fighting forces ever seen. Among the many tests they undergo is one where they are dropped off alone in the bush without any arms or ammunition, a match and material to strike it, and an egg. Lions, buffalo and elephant abound and the object is to have the egg hard-boiled and ready for inspection the following morning.

A Rhodesian Journalist sketched the Scouts' operational record briefly: Shrouded in secrecy with a mystique that spawns a thousand stories, many true and most mere rumour, the Scouts have in only two years become the most-decorated outfit in the

Rhodesian security forces collecting along the way amongst many other awards - six Silver Crosses (the highest award for gallantry yet presented); 11 Bronze Crosses; six orders for Members of the Legion of Merit for acts of bravery, seldom reported, but which have all played a major part in fighting the country's terror war. The Selous Scouts is fully integrated, with an undisclosed number of soldiers - but the ratio is eight Blacks to two White troops. The initial selection procedures last for about 18 days and are probably the most rigorous in the world. Every man who goes to the camp is a volunteer - and many are highly experienced, battle-hardened soldiers who find that after a few days they simply cannot stand the strain. Small wonder then that on the most recent selection course, only 14 out of 126 volunteers made the grade.

The officer commanding the Selous Scouts, and the driving force behind it, is Major Ron Reid-Daly, a 47-year-old regular soldier who was once regimental Sergeant- Major of the Rhodesian Light Infantry, known as "The Incredibles." He learned his job with the British Special Air Service in Malaya after leaving his native Salisbury in 1950 to go to England, and he served with the SAS during the Communist terror war there in the early 1950's.

The prison camp analogy does not elude Reid-Daly. I reckon in most armies today I simply wouldn't be allowed to put these poor bastards through the kind of selection course we give them. They'd think I was trying to kill the men who volunteer to join us. I agree, there is something of the prison camp attitude towards our men under selection and training. We take them to the very threshold of tolerance mentally - and it's here that most of them crack. You can take almost any fit man and train him to a high standard of physical ability. But you can't give a man what he hasn't already got inside him. Under selection each man is reduced to below a threshold, which the average human being could not endure. He is virtually "dehumanised", forced to live off rats, snakes, baboon meat and eyes, to survive in hostile surroundings, which prove that nature, too, can be as deadly as any human enemy. And they are taught to live off nature, to drink from the water in the carcass of a dead animal - a yellowish liquid - and to eat maggot-ridden green meat, which can be cooked only once before becoming deadly poisonous. Recruits are not given rations except for water. They are expected to survive off the land, making their own fires without matches, and making and using bark string - "gusi tambo" – to help catch food for themselves. They are soon hungry enough to capture any small creatures they can find - grasshoppers, lizards and squirrels - to stave off the hunger. "And you do get hungry." said one student who had recently been on the survival course. "We caught and killed a small leguaan, and before we even had time to skin it, one of the men was ready to take a bite out of it".

The Selous Scouts have for the first time admitted that they have been used on hot pursuit raids into Mozambique including the highly spectacular and tactically successful raid on the Nyadzonya terrorist training camp last August in which over 300, and possibly more than 500, terrorists were killed. For those who come through the selection course there follows a posting to one of the small sections on operations, after a short tracking course, initially as a flank tracker. They work in remote parts of Rhodesia hunting down terrorist spoor and leading the infantry in for the kill if the invading group is too big for the small two or three man teams to handle on their own. Each member of the Selous Scouts, down to the lowest ranking White soldier, speaks at least one African language - necessary for communication with their Black comrades-in-arms with whom they work in the closest possible context as equals. Tracking survival and close-combat tactics are high on the list of the Scout's training priorities. From what newsmen saw at Wafa Wafa camp it takes a very special kind of man to qualify for service in what has become Rhodesia's elite and much-envied military unit. Yet Major Reid-Daly detests the word elite: We do not consider ourselves an elite group of men, nor do we think we are of the highest calibre. It could cause the men to imagine themselves better than they really are and this could in turn lead to recklessness. We are simply just trackers out to do a job.

About training procedures, Major Reid-Daly, as tough as they come, explained:

We take a chap right down when he first comes here, right to the bottom. And then we build him up again into what we need in the Selous Scouts. Some people might say it's a dehumanising process, and maybe it is. But as far as I'm concerned, that's the way it has to be if we have to keep this unit up to standard. I have heard of all sorts of so-called crack outfits becoming nothing more than shadows of what they were because of a lowering of standards to increase the numbers of men going through into combat. And I'm determined not to let that happen here. You see these men sometimes in town, with their chocolate-brown berets and green belts with an osprey badge. The osprey is a bird of prey, a fish eater, not common, but found in small numbers in many parts of the world where there are large stretches of water. The badge - previously the unofficial badge of Rhodesia's tracking men - was drawn up in commemoration of Andre Rabie, the first regular instructor of tracking. He was killed on active service in 1973. Most of the men who are involved in this anti-terror outfit regard Andre Rabie as having being the inspiration behind the Selous Scouts.

The Selous Scouts have one of the best-stocked aviaries in Rhodesia. They have also added a snake park. Not as frivolous as it sounds. The emphasis is on bush survival and in order to survive for many days at a time if necessary, the men must be able to recognise and make use of whatever vegetation, birds, animals and insects the bush has to offer. They must also learn to understand and turn to advantage what they see. An instructor said: Everything is of some use to you in the veldt. The more you get familiar with it, the better your chance of survival. The ignorant person bumbles into trouble wherever he goes. Certain birds give your presence away. Butterflies, which some people see as nothing but pretty little insects, are a potent indication of water in the winter months. We aim to make our students at home in the environment in which they work. Vegetation not only provides them with food in times of need. It plays one of the basic roles in tracking. And certain trees are used medically. The marula gives the best anti-histamine you can find. Many of the men are trained parachutists to enable them to reach an area quickly when their tracking skills are required.

Their stories of survival in the bush are manifold - like the youngster from Salisbury who spent 18 days in the bush trying to evade a terrorist gang who were hot after his trail. As the Scout put it, "a spot of bother when something didn't work out quite right.

These are the men the terrorists want out of the way, men who are justifiably proud of their official motto – "Pamwe Chete", (Together Only or All together)

OBITUARY

Lieutenant Colonel Ronald "Ron" Francis Reid-Daly CLM, DMM, MBE.

On the 9th August 2010.

This great man Lieutenant Colonel Ronald "Ron" Francis Reid-Daly CLM, DMM, MBE.
The Founding Commander of the special force unit the Selous Scouts passed away at his home in Simon's Town, South Africa, after a long and bravely fought battle with cancer.

He was the Founding Commanding Officer of the Selous Scouts,
President of the Selous Scouts Regimental Association
Patron of the Rhodesian Light Infantry Regimental Association

22 September 1928 - 9 August 2010

"Gone Ishe' but never forgotten"

Appendix II
The Light at the End of the Tunnel

Sketch by Julie McDermott

BY
AUBREY BROOKS

Author's note

This is the story of an attempted coup d'etat more than 20 years ago on the Seychelles, an idyllic but obscure group of islands in the Indian Ocean. At the time the attempt made headlines across the world, partly because it involved names still famous/notorious from the mercenary involvement in the Congo in the 1960s; partly because it involved the hijacking of an Air India jet liner; partly because South Africa the international pariah was involved; and partly because the incident was perceived as another small skirmish in the Cold War.

However, this is more than a behind the scenes account of those faded headlines. It is the story of one individual's personal growth. I was wounded and captured in the Seychelles. I was severely beaten on a daily basis; stood trial then was sentenced to death. I eventually served two and a half years in prison, a time, which I value with hindsight because I now realise it was then, that I discovered hidden depths in my comrades and myself. I discovered humanity in my jailers and in the President of the Seychelles, who my group had set out to depose. Cut off from my wife and family, I treasured their support from a distance and today do not for an instant take for granted the strength and joy of a loving family. And I deepened my religious faith, which today lights my path. It seems an odd thing to say, but I owe a lot to that escapade in the Seychelles.

I realised how shallow and crass the racial attitudes are that exist in this world we live in. Human courage and kindness, I discovered, knows of no racial barriers. I experienced the unbelievable magnanimity and greatness of spirit of President Albert René, the man to whom I owe my life. I also experienced support from a distance from Archbishop Desmond Tutu, a person I had been conditioned to expect nothing from except hostility. It was an illuminating and humbling experience.

I also experienced the fickleness of the apartheid regime. I suppose it would have been expecting a bit much for them to admit they backed the Seychelles attempt, and supplied the weaponry, but as far as I am aware they subsequently did not stir a finger, officially or unofficially, to ameliorate our condition or secure our release. What they did do was put sinister and unpleasant pressure on my wife, alone in Durban with two young children, for reasons I am still at a loss to understand.

I was a soldier, and yes, a mercenary. Like most Rhodesians and South Africans of the day, I did have military experience. I had served with the Selous Scouts and the Grey Scouts, two elite units in the Rhodesian Bush War. I make no apology for that, as I believed at the time that I was fighting a just cause (some people say that UDI may have been a mistake, current events in Zimbabwe suggest we were not wrong). Like many Rhodesians and South Africans, broke and at a loose end in the early 1980s, I was available for recruitment to a mercenary force directed against a socialist (for that read communist in the idiom of the day) who had illegally seized power from a democratically elected president and now threatened to tilt the balance of power against the West in the Indian Ocean.

As I say, my views have since mellowed. I will probably never fully support the socialist principles of President René, but I can concede that he has a point here and there. Also, he is now democratically elected. Add to that his personal integrity and character and you have a remarkable personality. The erasure of racial prejudice from my mindset makes the new South Africa a vibrant and exciting place in which to be, with great possibilities.

More than 20 years later, I believe the time is right for me to publish this little booklet in the hope that it may touch, inspire or help someone who may take these written words and find them beneficial. It is my sincere hope too that by reading this booklet it will show you that a belief in your God, whoever he may be or even a belief in a superior being, added to a positive outlook and a firm belief in yourself, everything is possible. Over the years I have found that I personally embrace all religion and a wide variety of beliefs from other cultures.

I hope that some of your questions, fears and wishes may be answered through the pages of this little booklet. I also give thanks to my family, many friends and loved ones, who not only supported me then, but do so now.

Now these many years later I look back on a truly blessed life, where I have been given marvellous opportunities to travel around the world extensively, partake in ocean yacht racing, run many sporting events, climb Sydney Harbour Bridge, and be involved in a generally fun filled and exciting life, filled with adventure and no limit of where we can go.

Aubrey Brooks
Durban, South Africa
May 2006

THE STORY

I wrote this little booklet whilst I was still in prison under a death sentence for my participation in an attempted coup. I have put pen to paper in the hope that I can let others know what wonderful comfort and strength I have found in the scriptures. In order to show you how great Our Father's love is for us I must take you back to the start of my saga. It was a Wednesday evening at about 5:30pm, our operation was a failure and four of us were sent to an army camp to ensure that the entrance was blocked and that no one would be able to leave the camp.

Shortly after arrival at the camp I was involved with an exchange of firing with some soldiers and I was shot in the right leg, it started bleeding badly and we made our way up a small hill near the camp and in the course of the evening I was parted from my companions and so started a series of events which have clearly (indicated) proved to me beyond any doubt that we have a truly Great, Wonderful, Loving and Living God. I say Living God, because it is my belief that too many of us do not realise that Our Lord Jesus and Our Father do hear and answer our prayers. It is my firm belief that if we take the Scriptures literally, believe God's word and act on it

Our Father and Our Lord Jesus are always there waiting to show us their Great Love, Forgiveness and Mercy.

I spent Wednesday night out in the forest alone, in the rain and with a badly bleeding leg. My shirt was used as a tourniquet, which slowed the bleeding down to some extent, but there was also an extra hazard and that was shock. I fell on my knees and prayed to Our Father for strength and protection and shortly afterwards the first of many prayers were answered, the bleeding almost stopped, and I felt very calm, although I was only dressed in a pair of shorts and shoes, I felt very comforted.

I spent the next day up in the hills and late Thursday evening I came down the hill and was captured. Upon being arrested, I was handcuffed with my hands behind my back and also hog-tied, after a beating I was taken out to be shot and while I was being carried out I said the Lord's Prayer. I there asked for forgiveness for my sins (and here I am certain this is the Key that opens up the riches of this wonderful world that we live in) and asked Our Lord to please make peace with my family for me, to let them know that I loved them and that I did not mean to bring them any heartache and sorrow. I was then quite calm and suddenly a most miraculous thing happened, all the kicking and punching stopped, there was a shout and next minute I was taken back into my cell. If anyone had have been witnessing what had happened, they would have realised that it was nothing short of a miracle. Well when I was back in my cell, I realised beyond any doubt, that not only had my prayers been answered, but I had in fact been forgiven my sins right there and then, not I would be forgiven my sins if I did so and so, or maybe I would be forgiven my sins when such and such happened; no, my sins were forgiven there and then, as it says in Jeremiah 31vs34 *"I will forgive their sins and I will no longer remember their wrongs."* I believe that the Lord meant what He said and that on that night he forgave there and then. We must learn to accept the scriptures as Gospel and not question them. God did not put all of that into the Book for nothing. From that night on my prayer life changed dramatically, for although I used to pray on some occasions before (mostly when I was in trouble or in need) I did so only half expecting my prayers to be answered and even then a lot of my prayers were answered, but having had that wonderful experience on that night 2 November, I looked upon my prayer live in a new light and as it says in Mark 11vs24 when Jesus said *"For this reason I tell you when you pray and ask for something, believe that you have received it, and you will be given whatever you ask for".*

So we have been told what to do therefore we must not doubt, but believe and since then all my prayers have been answered and sometimes even more that I had prayed for. I remember whilst we were awaiting our trial we were taken to the police station on our return from court after being remanded and the evening before I had prayed earnestly to Our Lord that I may be allowed to write a short note home to my family, just to let them know that I was alright and to find out if they were alright. On arriving at the police station the Commissioner of Police took me up to his office and enquired as to why my family had not made contact with me, upon hearing my thoughts about the situation, he then asked me if I had a telephone at home, when I replied yes, he place a call through to my wife and minutes later I was talking to her. This once again showed me that nothing is impossible for Our Lord and that he is just waiting to show us his Great Love for us and that it is us who complicate our prayer life for Him. We are so fortunate; we have someone to call on at anytime, day and night, under any circumstances and with no preconditions, for Us Our Lord say in: John 6vs37 "Everyone whom my Father gives me will come to me. I will never turn away anyone who comes to me". So let us take Our Lord at His Word and place all our trust and faith in Him, for He tells us in no uncertain terms that he will not turn us away so accept it, what more could we want?

Our Lord could not be more explicit than that could He? Let us go to Him. He is just waiting to help us, to show us His Great Love for us, all we need do is ask.

In the months that followed, I had many prayers answered and these were all answered in the most difficult conditions. For 9 months we were placed in solitary confinement and the first 5 months we were allowed no reading material at all, in fact not even a Bible. In our cell, all we had was only one bed, one sheet, one pillow, one pillowcase, one towel and only one pair of shorts to wear so one can imagine to have prayers answered in those conditions was no mean feat, as we were only allowed out to the toilet for a total of approximately 20 minutes a day, but Our Lord did hear our prayers and they were answered. In the 9th month of our confinement and extraordinary thing happened, the army camp where we were detained mutinied and during the course of events that followed, the guards who were looking after us, ran off and left us locked in our cells this was due to the fact that our camp was being mortared and fired on by loyal troops.

If you could now imagine the position we were in, our cells were on the top floor of the prison and we had a concrete roof over us, which gave some protection against a mortar bomb, but one of our group had only asbestos and timber which gave no protection at all. We were mortared over a two day period by 40-50 bombs which fell all around us and not one of us were injured at all, in fact during the early hours of our second morning of being attacked, the same chap managed to escape from his cell and release the rest of us. We then locked ourselves up in the kitchens which were below our cells and sat out the rest of the incident. During the Mortaring I would lie flat on the floor of my cell with my Bible and read out of the book of Psalms and looking back on that period, now I have no doubt in my mind that the Lord was with us and that He protected us through all that, as I was totally calm and at peace throughout.

What I am trying to say in these pages of print here is that I am certain in my mind that it would be impossible to put down all the good things that happened to us and the incredible protection that we enjoyed, to luck or circumstances for there were too many occasions and under such extreme conditions for it to be labelled as such, no, I know in my heart that the Good Lord was with us, that He heard our prayers and was right there with us for as John 3vs15 reads *"So that everyone who believes in Him may not die but have eternal life",* you see it is in the scriptures, so do not doubt, just Believe.

Earlier on in the booklet, I mentioned that I had found the key to our prayers being answered, and of this I am certain, for as we see in Romans 10vs9-11, *"If you confess that Jesus is Lord and believe that God raised him from death you will be saved".*

For it is by our faith that we are put right with God; it is by our confession that we are saved. The scripture says, "Whoever puts his trust in Him will not be put to shame." So we can see that it is by faith that we are saved. I know what it has done for me and I hope that you will also benefit from my experience.

Paul tells us in Romans 3vs23 *"Everyone has sinned and is far away from God's savings presence".* That may sound quite frightening and very final, but that is not where it ends, for God has shown us the way to be put right and He wants all of mankind to be put right, yes, He loves us all equally, He has no favourites so all we have to do is: Recognise that we are sinners and that we are lost without God: Repent, truly repent: and ask for forgiveness.

God will answer us, He wants us all to be saved so go ahead do it, believe from your heart and confess with your mouth that God does forgive you of your sins and that He does cleanse you from all unrighteousness and you will see a whole new life open up before you, a new and wonderful life with our Lord.

During our months of solitary confinement I also discovered another very important thing and that is that no Christian can ever be placed in solitary confinement. Now that seems to be a bold statement, but it is true, for every Christian has the Lord with Him, therefore you are two, and so you see solitary confinement does not exist. In those months our Lord did so much for me that it would fill many pages if I were to write all that was done for me but, I would like to illustrate to you the extent of our Father's Great Love for us. During the time of our confinement I was longing to hear some news from my daughter, who was from a previous marriage, and whom I had not heard from for about 11 years.

I prayed to our Father and told him that I just longed to know if she was alright as she was constantly on my mind and that I was worried about her. About a little while later I got a letter from my wife saying that out of the blue, my daughter had phoned her and that she had come to spend the weekend with my wife and two sons and that was not all, for our daughter had got married and had now come to live in South Africa not far from our home, they were now in regular telephonic contact every week and that they spend as least one weekend a month together. Once again Our Father answered my prayers and the comfort that comes from having your prayers answered is really something else, it is wonderful to know that our Father does hear our prayers and that He do answer them.

I have found such great comfort in the Book of Psalms, one Psalm that comes to mind for comfort and strength and which tells us that Our Lord is always with us is Psalm 73vs 23-26, *"Yet I always stay close to you, and you hold me by the hand you guide me with your instruction and at the end you will receive me with Honour. What else have I in Heaven but you? Since I have you, what else could I want on Earth? My mind and my body may grow weaker, but God is my strength; He is all I ever need".*

And in fact that is all you ever do need for my Bible and my faith have brought me through what would have been a very trying and difficult time.

I would not be telling the truth if I said that there were not times when I got anxious and worried but we were sent a little booklet that was written by an Evangelist "Kenneth E Hagin", the booklet was entitled "Praying To Get Results" and chapter 3 of his book is entitled "You don't have to worry" in this book he quotes : Philippians 4vs6 *"Don't worry about anything, but in all your prayers ask God for what you need, always ask Him with a thankful heart"*, and again in 1Peter 5vs7 *"Leave all your worries with Him because He cares for you"*. Yet again in Matthew 6vs25-27 *"This is why I tell you not to be worried about the food and drink you need in order to stay alive, or about clothes for your body. After all isn't life worth more that food? And isn't the body worth more than clothes? Look at the birds flying around, they do not sow seeds, gather a harvest and put it in barns; yet your Father in Heaven takes care of them! Aren't you worth much more than birds?"*

Can any of you live a bit longer by worrying about it and verse 33 and 34 tells us *"Instead be concerned above everything else with the Kingdom of God and with what he requires of you and He will provide you with all the other things"*. So do not worry about tomorrow, it will have enough worries of its own.

There is no need to add to the troubles each day brings. There we have it, we are told what to do, so lets do it, I did and I have never looked back, yes I cast my worries and problems onto our Lord just as we are told to and I have never looked back. You may say how can I do this when I am still in prison with a death sentence over my head? Well, let me explain to you. You see, I have accepted the Word as Gospel and I have not doubt in my mind at all as in Ephesians 1vs11 *"All things are done according to God's plan and decision; and God chose us to be his own people, in union with Christ because of his own purpose, based on what He had decided from the very beginning. Let us then, who were the first to hope in Christ, praise God's Glory"*, and again in Ephesians 2vs10 *"God has made us what we are, and in our Union with Christ Jesus He has created us for a life of good deeds, which He has already prepared for us to do"*. As you can see, the scriptures have told me that there is a reason for being here and also that Our God has work for me to do still and so it is with this knowledge and my faith that I can, and do look forward to a wonderful future with Our Lord. I believe in my heart that Our Lord has forgiven me my sins and that one-day I will be reunited with my family and starting a new life with Our Lord.

TIME: 10:00pm

Day: Saturday 9th April 1983

<u>PRAYED TO</u>

Photo: Jo Torrien

Aubrey Brooks served in the Rhodesian Army for 19 years, both in the Rhodesian Armed Forces (including the Mounted Horse Unit, the Grey's Scouts and the Special Forces unit the Selous Scouts).

He has enjoyed the adventurous side of life, and has raced both motorcars and motorcycles, and holds a private pilot's licence.

When he went to the Seychelles with Col. Mike Hoare's mercenaries in 1981, he was captured and sentenced to death for Treason (it was during this time while in solitary confinement that this booklet was written) He was granted a full Presidential pardon 22 months later and is now reunited with his wife and family.

Appendix III
The Truth Commission Files

Extracts taken from the case of the "Seychelles" report:

The Case of the "Seychelles"

The Truth Commission Files

[Seych-Report]
Date (coup attempt): 25th November 1981

Place: Mahé International Airport on Mahé Island (Seychelles)

Name Victim:
Objective of the coup was to bring down the Seychelles government of President France-Albert René and to re-install the former President James Mancham

Information Victim:
President France-Albert René: he ousted the former President Mancham in the 1977 coup [SE: 167]. Mancham had been 'enthusiastically wooed by former information Secretary Eschel Rhoodie as a politically ally' and SA was unhappy with the rule of René. After the overthrow of Mancham, SA aircraft landing rights were withdrawn and SA'n economic overtures collapsed. [S.Tribune 29/11/81]

Perpetrators:
Hoare and his 43 mercenaries (Notes*1) were disguised as tourists: rugby players and members of a beer-drinking group called the "Ancient Order of Froth blowers." They arrived in a Royal Swazi jet on Mahé, carrying their own weapons. Nine mercs (members of Hoare's advance guard) were already on the island on the evening of Wednesday, 25th November 1981.

Perpetrators information:
In 1978 Seychelles exiles in SA, acting on behalf of ex-president James Mancham, began discussions with officials concerning a coup attempt to be launched in Seychelles. [SE: 172] Gérard Hoareau, Seychelle dissident, was one of the authors

of the 1981 coup attempt. Later expelled from SA. - As coup plans developed, the operation became an object of struggle between the Military Intelligence service (MI) and the civilian one (NIS). The SA Government allocated the coup operation to MI, but appointed Martin Dolinchek as a liaison officer on behalf of the NIS. [SE: 173] - Operation entrusted to Mike Hoare ('Mad Mike' Hoare), an Irish mercenary soldier (ex-Congo) living in SA as a civilian. Among the 53 people selected to carry out the coup: some members of the SA special forces (Recces), several former Rhodesian soldiers and ex-Congo mercs. [SE: 173; Mockler: 284-294]

Crime activity:
Coup attempt. The coup attempt was unexpectedly triggered off when an alert customs official spotted an AK-47 assault rifle in the luggage of one of the mercs [RDMail 13/4/82]. The invaders fought a brief gun-battle at the airport and 45 live mercenaries escaped aboard an Air India jet (Air India Boeing aircraft Flight 224) which happened to be on the tarmac and which they hijacked. One merc had died during the skirmish. Five soldiers, a female accomplice and also Martin Dolinchek (alias Anton Lubic) were left behind. [Mockler: 311] The mercs took some hostages, who were later freed unharmed. A police sergeant was wounded and an army 2nd Lieutenant David Antat was killed.

Crime Results:
The Seychelles Govt. arrested the seven (6 men and 1 woman) who remained on the Seychelles and tried the men (June-July 1982). The charges against the woman were dropped. Four of the six were sentenced to death (Brooks, Carey, England and Puren). Dolinchek was sentenced to 20 years, imprisonment and Sims to 10. After negotiations, all were eventually returned to SA in mid-1983. - In January 1982 an International Commission, appointed by the UN Security Council, made an inquiry of this mercenary aggression. -Hoare and his mercenaries (45 in total) were tried on their return to South Africa, but not for having attempted to organize a coup in a foreign country. The accused were charged before court with specific offences under the Civil Aviation Offences Act of 1972. [Argus 27/7/82]. The judge concluded that the SA Govt. was not involved in the Seychelles affair [Argus 27/6/82]. Hoare got 10 years, Peter Duffy, Mike Webb, Tullio Moneta and Pieter Doorewaard (probably the most senior of the Recce Commando reservists) were sentenced to 5 years, Ken Dalgliesh to 1 year, and Charles Goatley to 2 1/2 years. [Mockler: 330]; the other mercs (39) were freed [F&R: 1981-Z22]. -Pretoria Govt. embarrassed, opened negotiations for the return of the 6 arrested men. SA Govt. paid President René a ransom of $ 3 million (of which his cabinet was not informed) and came to a broader understanding with Pres. René personally [SE: 173] -Beset by attention of foreign secret services and by plots of within, Pres. René asked his friend, the Italian businessman Mario Ricci (Notes:*2) to help improve his security service [SE: 174]. He realized that he needed to adjust his foreign policy to accommodate SA interests,

at least in some measure. -In the aftermath of the 1981 coup attempt SA secret services came fully to appreciate Ricci's significance as a potential intermediary with President René. SA "super-spy' Craig Williamson (notes*3) developed in the mid-1980s a close relationship with Ricci. [SE: 175]

Crime Motives:
1. Seychelles was of considerable strategic interest to the USA, USSR, France, South Africa and others, all of which sought to exercise influence in this islands.
   After 1979 (when SA's main supply of oil was threatened) Seychelles had a minor but distinct role to play in the new strategy of the 'total onslaught'. The islands offered a) potential military facilities and b) could possibly be used as a base for clandestine trading purposes in the face of economic sanctions (after the Iranian revolution of 1979 especially oil). SA was unhappy with the rule of President René, far to the left of his predecessor. So, a coup was planned [SE: 172-3] with the objective, to bring down the government of President René and install Mr. Mancham (the former President) [F&R81:Z22].
2. [RDMail:13/4/82]: the long term aim in overthrowing the Seychelles Government was to have a base from which the Tanzanian Government could be destabilized, Mr. Dolinchek said. Other reasons included landing rights for SAA aircraft and a strategic base on the important Cape sea route. It was said [Argus 27/7/82] that the American CIA were sympathetic and that the American and Kenyan Governments would give instant recognition to the reinstated Seychelles Government.

Chain of Command:
Prime Minister P.W. Botha emphasized that the attempted coup was carried out without the knowledge of the Government, the Cabinet or the State Security Council and that no authorization was given. Also the judge in the hijack-trial concluded that the SA Govt. was not involved in Seychelles affair [Argus 27/6/82] - [RDMail: 4/5/82]: Hoare said that the Cabinet and top ranking officers of the NIS and the SADF knew about and condoned the abortive Seychelles coup. His initial contact with the NIS had been through Mr. Martin Dolinchek. Through him Hoare arranged meetings with Mr. Van Wyk (BOSS, forerunner of the NIS) who said he would submit a minute to the Cabinet of the proposals to take the Seychelles by force. The initial approach failed. Later he had met with Mr. N.J. (James Younger) Claasen of NIS (Deputy Director and Dolinchek's handler) who informed Hoare that the Cabinet had given their approval in principle. Mr. Claasen introduced Hoare to Brigadiers Hamman and Knoetze. Hoare gave them the details of the plans which were studied at length. The men acceded to the request for arms and ammunition and radios. Hoare submitted as evidence an invoice, purportedly from the SADF certifying the delivery to the home of weapons and ammunition to be

used in the coup (75 AK-47 assault rifles, nearly 24,000 rounds of ammunition, 40 hand grenades and 100 rockets [The Guardian(Br), 4/5/82]. Military Intelligence was prepared to back the coup. But, it was a question of keeping South African involvement to a minimum. -Mercs like Beck claimed that Hoare had told them that the coup was officially backed. -Mr. Martin Dolinchek (alias Anton Lubic) declared that his department (NIS) and the SADF had full and prior knowledge of the coup plans. The coup plans were put to the SA Govt. in 1979 and rejected, only to be accepted in 1980 with the logistical support given by the SADF in the form of weapons (AK-47 assault rifles; other weapons would be available on the island). [RDMail -13-14/4/82]. Dolinchek named Major General Charles Lloyd, an officer commanding South West African security forces, as a man with intimate prior knowledge of the bungled Seychelles coup. Lloyd was an SADF recipient of a report written by Dolinchek on the Seychelles invasion plan as presented by Colonel 'Mad Mike' Hoare in 1980. It was before Lloyd was appointed OC in SWA. The report had also been given to his own department (NIS). He had travelled to the Seychelles on a SA passport (no. D631473) as 'Anton Lubic'. It was issued on 12/10/81 by his contact (Mrs. Van Heerden) in the Department of the Interior in Durban.

Witnesses:

1. Key witnesses of the Maritzburg hijack trial included the Air India pilot: Captain Umesh Saxena and Seychellois officials who negotiated with the mercenaries during the short-lived invasion [BD 15/1/82]; Third Defence Force reconnaissance unit doctor Dr. Christiaan Lodewicus De Jager was giving evidence for the State; two Recce coleagues Dr. Steyn De Wet and Dr. Theodorus Van Huyssteen (never called) have turned State witness in the trial and gained indemnity against prosecution [NP 19/3/82].2. [RDMail:13/4/82]: the long term aim in overthrowing the Seychelles Government was to have a base from which the Tanzanian Government could be destabilized, Mr. Dolinchek said. Other reasons included landing rights for SAA aircraft and a strategic base on the important Cape Sea route. It was said [Argus 27/7/82] that the American CIA were sympathetic and that the American and Kenyan Governments would give instant recognition to the reinstated Seychelles Government.

2. Mr. Martin Dolinchek (see above).

3. Mr. Mike Hoare (see above).

Notes:
*1 Names of mercenaries involved in the attempted 1981 coup in the Seychelles. There were 54 mercenaries involved (1 deserted, 1 died):
Name, Military Background, Arrived in Durban / remained in the Seychelles, Remarks.

BOTES, Desmond (Des) Jurgens - probably ex-Congo merc; once in the Rhod. Police (Sp. Branch) Durban, Advance guard; once SA's karate champ; karate-school Jo'burg.

BROOKS, Aubrey formerly Selous Scouts, Rhod. Seychelles Zimbabwean Advance guard; wounded; Treason charge; Age: 38 y.

CAREY, Bernard (Barney), probably ex-Congo and Yemen merc, Seychelles, British; lived, in SA (since 1980: repairs business P. Maritzburg). Advance guard; Treason charge; Age: 39 y.

DALGLEISH, Kenneth Hugh once in the Rhod. Police (Sp. Branch) Durban Advance guard; took charge with Mr. Duffy of the negotiations in Durb; Maritzburg trial: 2 1/2y.

DOLINCHEK, Martin, (alias Anton Lubic) NIS Seychelles Liaison officer on behalf of the NIS; Advance guard; Treason charge: 20 y. He lived under the name Martin Donaldson in Durban.

DUFFY, Peter ex-Congo merc Durban, Durban news photographer; karate expert; 'tour leader' of the beer drinking club; took charge of negotiations in Durban together with DALGLIESH; Maritzburg trial: 5 y.

DUKES, Charles William, SADF (Malan); ex-SAS/ Rhod. ex-1 Recce Commando, Durban American merc Advance guard; Wounded during attack on army barracks.

ENGLAND, Roger ex 3rd Para's (Angola merc era); ex-Rhod. SAS, Seychelles Zimbabwean - Advance guard; Treason trial.

HOARE, Thomas Michael (alias Mr. Thomas Boarel) ex-Congo merc Durban Col. "Mad Mike" Hoare; Irish merc living in SA; Head of the operation; Maritzburg trial: 10 y; Age: 63.

INGLE, Susan (alias Mrs. SIMS), civilian Seychelles British-born Advance guard; "Wife" of Bob SIMS, Charges dropped.

PUREN, Jeremiah (Jerry) ex-Congo merc Seychelles Afrikaner; 2nd hand car business in Durban; Treason trial; Age: 57.

SIMS, Robert (Bob), civilian Seychelles Advance guard (together with Mrs. INGLE); brother of Mike Hoare's wife Phillis; Profession: jockey and trainer; charged: illegally importing arms; Age: 49.

54 mercs:
Unknown: 7.
SADF: 27 (included: also Congo: 1; Congo/Rhod: 1; Rhod: 2).
Ex-Congo merc: 7 (included: also Yemen: 1).
Ex-Rhod. Unit: 9 (included: also Congo: 1).
NIS: 1.
Civilian: 3.
Defected: 1 Died: 1 Seychelles: 7 Durban: 45.
16 had been or were a member of a Rhod. Unit or lived in Zimbabwe; all the others are South Africans or lived in SA.

Remarks:

1. Persons (25) mentioned in the Gen. Malan affidavit (Malan) were almost certainly members or former members of the SADF (see Cape Times 17/June/1982).

2. DE BEER, Johannes (Vic) Lodewikus Pretorius (or PRETORIUS) could be an important operator: he managed to keep 'clean', although he was a lieutenant in One Recce Commando and responsible for issuing the call-up papers of the Recces involved.

3. I didn't find Ronald Desmond BEZUIDENHOUT (alias Duncan Smith-in the ANC-, alias Tokaref) who participated also in the coup (probably under another name) [VW].

4. See RDMail 12/3/82; TRC Seychelles Hit 25/6/96; Mockler, 1985 "Paradise Lost- Coup in the Seychelles & Trials and Tribulations" pp.284-350; Cape Times 17/June/ 1982; Hoare;. *2 Giovanni Mario Ricci (born in Italy 1929) lived since 1974 in the Seychelles where he became an important intermediary for foreigners [SE: 169]. He became René's friend and unofficial financial advisor. He was associated with some very unusual companies as: the 'Seychelles Trust Company'/ SETCO (since 1978) through which he masterminded the establishment of the Seychelles as a tax haven; the 'International Monetary Funding', or IMF (1982, not to be confused with the International Monetary Fund/IMF) and the commercial company 'Order of the Coptic Catholic Knights of Nalta'(1984, not to be confused with the well-known Vatican order) through which Ricci, got a diplomatic status. He used his company GMR (named after his own initials), as a flagship for various interests. By early 1980s Ricci acquired a reputation as someone who could be approached by anyone who wished to transact some form of business in Seychelles [SE: 169-171]. Ricci is considered as the Mafia's key figure in the Seychelles [ION-209, 7/12/95]. Ricci greeted Francesco Pazienza in the Seychelles, in 1983, when the latter had to flee Italian justice. It was Pazienza who introduced SASEA/ 'Société Anonyme Suisse

d'Exportations Agricoles' (headed by Florio Fiorini) into the Seychelles. Pazienza's name has been associated with several major scandals. [SE: 183-184] and the same counts for SASEA and its sub-companies. The Seychelles tax haven is one of the most attractive in the world (ION: 486 6/7/91). It is a 'private' one, entirely controlled by Mario Ricci's SETCO. He was also in charge of Seychellois external intelligence operations: surveillance of the opposition, installing telephone bugs in France and Great Britain [Intelligence Newsletter 1/3/89]. Ricci faces trial in France (1987) charged with 'criminal association and infringement of privacy' for ordering the tapping of the telephone of Seychelles's opposition leader Gérard Hoareau, who was murdered in London several months later (Nov.1985) [ION-209, 7/12/85]. Ricci, having become an embarrassment to the Seychelles, left the island in August 1986 to settle in South Africa where he joined forces with Craig Williamson. *3 Craig Williamson first, number 2 person in section A, the foreign desk of the South African Security Police and since 1985 a colonel in SA Military Intelligence came to appreciate the possibilities of the extraordinary empire built by Ricci. In 1986 Williamson became managing director of the South African subsidiary of Ricci's GMR Empire (GMR-South Africa). Williamson helped to set up a risk consultancy company called 'Longreach', an affiliate of GMR but in fact secretly owned by SA Military Intelligence for which it operated. Williamson admitted that this company had engaged a French mercenary to carry out the attempted murder of President Lennox Sebe of Ciskei. He has also arranged the import of a cargo of oil into SA via the Seychelles [Africa Confidential, vol.28 no.8; SE: 175-178].

Sources:
Ellis, Stephen: "Africa and international corruption: the strange case of South Africa and Seychelles" in African Affairs (1996), 95, pp.165-196.[SE:] -TRC-doc; Seychelles Hit, List of names 25/6/96 [TRC-list] -Pauw, Jacques: "Die grusame verhaal van sersant Ronald Bezuidenhout, alias Tokaref"; Vrije Weekblad, 17-23 Mei, 1991 [VW] -Mockler, Anthony: 'Paradise Lost - Coup in the Seychelles', ch. 13 & 'Trials and Tribulations', ch.14; pp. 284-348, in: (title unknown); Letchworth (Hertfordshire): The Garden City Press, 1985 [Mockler:] -Intelligence Newsletter [IN:]-Indian Ocean Newsletter [ION:] -Africa Confidential [AC:]-cuttings of SA and international newspapers - Mike Hoare: The Seychelles affair; New York: Bantam Press, 1986 207 pp.
White Paper on Aggression of November 25th 1981 against the Republic of Seychelles; Victoria: Seychelles National Printing Company Ltd., 265 pp.

Amsterdam Aug. 1996
The (secret) Truth Commission Files

Appendix IV
A Letter from Len Morison
The Story of Royal Swazi Airways Fokker F28

Manager South Africa
Royal Swazi Airways

Hello Aubrey
Long time no hear.
I hope that you and the family are well.
I have just finished reading your book. What a harrowing experience you and the others suffered at the hands of those cowardly Tanzanians. I am so glad that eventually you all came through that terrible ordeal.
I hope that you don't mind if I correct some inaccuracies in both your book and that of Col. Hoare.

Air Swaziland
As the photo in your book of the group arriving in Mahé shows, the name of the carrier is 'Royal Swazi'. We (Royal Swazi Airways) had been operating a twice-weekly service from Swaziland to Comoros and Seychelles since July 1981. Apart from our 60-seater Fokker F28 jet there were no aircraft of a suitable size available in Southern Africa that had the range to carry this group of 44. If there had been, the cost would have been prohibitive and a charter flight would have required South African and Seychelles DCA clearances causing unwanted attention.

Chapter 5
Moroni stopover – *Quote:* '…three passengers asked if there was enough space available on the aircraft to the Seychelles. It was felt that this could only add to the cover of the 'Froth-Blowers' mission.' *Unquote.*
   This implies that Col. Hoare had paid for the entire flight and that is incorrect. The group only paid for the seats they occupied. There were three other passengers plus the group that travelled from Swaziland. At Moroni, two passengers got off. The other passenger was a member of my staff who was under my instruction to meet hoteliers in Seychelles. In Moroni, only one other passenger got aboard. He was the one who had the plant that caused the upset at customs in Seychelles.

Travel Arrangements

As Col Hoare mentions in his book, he relied on a South African travel agent to make all the travel arrangements. At the time, only British Airways and Royal Swazi had flights from southern Africa to the Seychelles. Why they chose Royal Swazi I don't know. Maybe it was the price? But possibly it was because a group flying direct from South Africa with British Airways might have caused suspicion? The travel agency contacted me at Royal Swazi in Johannesburg on 11 November to book the group on our schedule flight of 25 November returning 10 December and I gave them a very good price.

They obviously did not tell Col Hoare of this as according to Page 22 of your book he told your group on 14 November that *Quote*: 'The main group were to arrive on a charter flight from Swaziland' *Unquote*. I wonder why?

Air India 224 Harare-Seychelles-Bombay

I agree that under normal circumstances the Air India 707 should have just had enough fuel to divert to Mombasa, Kenya when it approached Mahé on the evening of 25 November, but I tend to believe Captain Saxena that he *had* to land. Possibly they didn't fill up completely in Harare, as the fuel price was probably higher? But it is not uncommon for commercial aircraft to operate on a basis of 'point of no return' to maximise payload or due to short range.

The Aftermath:

Although I realise that your book is a personal account, nothing is mentioned in either book or official document (The Truth Commission Files) of the consequences this abortive coup had on Royal Swazi Airways. We were the innocent party in all this but we lost the most!

Our aircraft was machine-gunned and two RPG shot through the fuselage by rampant vengeful Tanzanian troops. Amazingly, it did not explode although it was refuelled for the next morning's schedule departure.

Our managing director and board of directors had to fly to the Seychelles to clarify our position with the government and a whole lot of diplomatic flurry ensued with other African and Indian Ocean states.

Royal Swazi Airways had operated on a very busy schedule since 1978 but had only one aircraft, the Fokker F28. Each week this aircraft flew a busy schedule operation between Swaziland and Johannesburg, Durban, Harare, Lusaka, Mauritius, Comoros, Seychelles.

After this catastrophic event, I managed to hire Comair F27 aircraft to operate on our behalf between Johannesburg and Swaziland but had to reroute all other passengers via Johannesburg onto other carriers, paying overnight hotel accommodation for passengers and losing an awful lot of revenue. I had to cancel all of our other flights until we could obtain replacement aircraft.

In the meantime we had full flights to Mauritius and Seychelles during the busy December holidays but now no aircraft!

I contacted South African Airways to hire any of their aircraft. They offered all sorts of excuses but no help.

Madagascar then cancelled our over-flying rights to Mauritius and Comoros had also refused our flights.

Air Malawi refused to assist due to our 'association' with the coup attempt!

My old friends in Air Zimbabwe couldn't help either.

As all SAA schedules were full, I tried to get them to provide supplementary flights to carry our Mauritius passengers. They couldn't.

I contacted Air Mauritius to help. They said that they had no crew but wouldn't object if I found another carrier to operate.

I contacted the only other airline with long-range equipment, 'Luxavia'. They agreed to help with their 707 but SAA and Air Mauritius opposed our application to SA DCA.

Such is the spiteful world of aviation politics! That's what happens when little guys get in the way of monopolistic big brother. Our little independent airline was almost destroyed. SAA did not get back their landing rights to Seychelles until there was a change in South Africa's government.

During the following year SAA eventually agreed to hire us an old B737, even painting it in our colours and we reinstated most of our original routes. Due to the political upheaval and the 737's short range, we replaced Mauritius, Comoros and Seychelles with a new route to Blantyre and Nairobi. However, operating the 737 was a loss making exercise.

As for our poor Fokker F28 lying at Mahé airport, Seychellois stripped the interior and avionics, even stealing the toilet unit. The aircraft rotted in the heat of the Seychelles for six months before the insurance company eventually agreed to send a team to cut off the wings and tail and fly them and the fuselage in two C130's to Amsterdam. The repair took another six months.

Having nurtured the growth of the airline from its inception, this incident was a terrible blow to me personally. But fortunately, when one door closed another opens and new ventures for the airline were later found in East Africa, Lesotho and Cape Town.

I do not bear a grudge but I cannot forget and your book brought it all back so vividly. I sincerely hope that your book is a great success. Maybe some of my comments can be added to the next print run.

All the best.

Your old Corp of Signals and racing buddy from the old Rhodesian days,

Len Morison
Manager South Africa
Royal Swazi Airways
Johannesburg
1978-1998

Other titles published by Helion & Company

BUSH WAR OPERATOR: MEMOIRS OF THE RHODESIAN LIGHT INFANTRY, SELOUS SCOUTS AND BEYOND
A J Balaam
288pp
Paperback
ISBN 978-1-909982-77-2

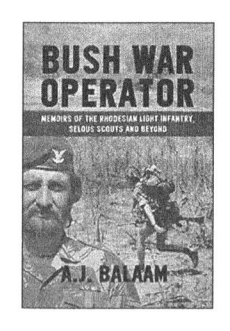

WEEP FOR AFRICA: A RHODESIAN LIGHT INFANTRY PARATROOPER'S FAREWELL TO INNOCENCE
Jeremy Hall
352pp
Paperback
ISBN 978-1-909982-33-8

FORTHCOMING TITLES

THE EQUUS MEN: RHODESIA'S MOUNTED INFANTRY: THE GREY'S SCOUTS 1896–1980
Alexandre Binda
224pp
Hardback
ISBN 978-1-910294-04-8

IF YOU GET YOURSELF KILLED, YOU'RE FIRED! THE EXTRAORDINARY LIFE OF AN ORDINARY REPORTER ON THE FRONT LINES OF AFRICA
Wilf Nussey
640pp
Paperback
ISBN 978-1-909982-54-3

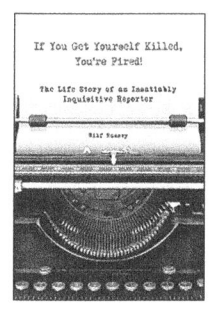